全国高职高专教育"十二五"规划教材

旅游与酒店英语

主　编　张志华　赵　楠

东南大学出版社
·南京·

图书在版编目(CIP)数据

旅游与酒店英语 / 张志华,赵楠主编. —南京：
东南大学出版社,2014.5
ISBN 978-7-5641-4681-8

Ⅰ. ①旅… Ⅱ. ①张… ②赵… Ⅲ. ①旅游服务—商业服务—英语—教材②饭店—商业服务—英语—教材
Ⅳ. ①H31

中国版本图书馆 CIP 数据核字(2013)第 291276 号

旅游与酒店英语

出版发行：东南大学出版社
社　　址：南京市四牌楼2号　邮编:210096
出 版 人：江建中
网　　址：http://www.seupress.com
经　　销：全国各地新华书店
印　　刷：南京师范大学印刷厂
开　　本：787mm×1092mm　1/16
印　　张：10.75
字　　数：250 千字
版　　次：2014 年 5 月第 1 版
印　　次：2014 年 5 月第 1 次印刷
印　　数：1—3000 册
书　　号：ISBN 978-7-5641-4681-8
定　　价：22.00 元

本社图书若有印装质量问题,请直接与营销部联系. 电话(传真):025-83791830

　　《旅游与酒店英语》是针对旅游与酒店管理专业及旅游英语专业培养应用型人才而编写的教材。本书适用于高职院校旅游与酒店专业、旅游英语专业的学生、旅游从业者、旅游英语自学者。

　　蓬勃发展的旅游业让笔者意识到，旅游专业人才的培养特别是优秀的涉外导游人员的培养是旅游教育的一项重要任务。随着市场经济的发展以及现代旅游业和酒店业的发展，该行业对酒店从业人员的需求量日益增多，对员工素质的要求也越来越高，促使我国旅游教育的规模不断扩大。职业院校旅游专业和酒店管理专业的学生已成为旅游服务业从业大军中的主要力量。因此，提高职业教育的教学质量，尤其是提高教材的质量，就显得日益重要。

　　本书主要有以下几个特色：

　　一是适应旅游酒店职业教育和职业培训发展的要求，突出职业教育以能力为本位，重视实践能力的培养。理论以够用为度，进一步加强了实践性教学内容，以满足旅游酒店从业人员和毕业生所从事职业的实际需要。

　　二是根据行业发展趋势，力求教材内容与时俱进。合理编写教材内容，尽可能多地在教材中充实新理念、新知识、新方法等方面内容，并力求贴合实际岗位的变化和新的要求，以便更好地提升旅游酒店从业人员的岗位竞争能力。

　　本书共计十二章，前六章由张志华老师负责完成，主要是旅游服务，包括旅游咨询、机场接机、地陪导游、旅游购物、休闲娱乐、处理问题与紧急情况等。后六章由赵楠老师负责完成，主要是酒店服务，包括酒店预订、前台接待、客房服务、前台结账、西餐厅、中餐厅等。全书内容包括背景知识、阅读、对话、功能句及扩展阅读。

　　本书在编写过程中，参阅了大量有关旅游和酒店管理的书籍和文献资料以及相关案例，在此谨向编著这些著作、资料的专家和学者致以诚挚的感谢！

　　由于时间仓促和编者水平有限，书中的不足在所难免，恳请各位专家和读者不吝指教，以期在日后修订再版时更正。

编　者
2013 年 9 月

Unit 1　Giving Travel Information ·················· 1
Unit 2　At the Airport ·················· 11
Unit 3　Local Tour Guide Service ·················· 22
Unit 4　Shopping ·················· 33
Unit 5　Entertainment ·················· 42
Unit 6　Handling Problems and Emergencies ·················· 54
Unit 7　Room Reservation ·················· 64
Unit 8　Reception Service ·················· 78
Unit 9　In-house Service ·················· 90
Unit 10　Check-out Service ·················· 102
Unit 11　A La Carte ·················· 113
Unit 12　In Chinese Restaurant ·················· 125
Vocabulary ·················· 138
参考文献 ·················· 164

Unit 1 Giving Travel Information

Unit Objectives

Master the basic words and expressions about travel information;
Get some cultural knowledge about travel abroad;
Know the advantages and disadvantages of different types of travel.

Background Knowledge

Top 10 Tips of Travel abroad

1. Check the latest travel advice for your **destination** and **subscribe** to receive free e-mail **notification** each time the travel advice for your destination is updated.

2. Take out appropriate travel insurance to cover hospital treatment, **medical evacuation** and any activities, including adventure sports, in which you plan to **participate**.

3. Before traveling overseas register your travel and contact details online or at the local **embassy**, **high commission** or **consulate** once you arrive, so we can contact you in an **emergency**.

4. Obey the law. Consular assistance cannot **override** local laws, even where local laws appear **harsh** or unjust by standards.

5. Check to see if you require visas for the country or countries you are visiting or **transiting**. Be aware that a visa does not guarantee entry.

6. Make copies of your passport details, insurance policy, traveler's cheques, visas and credit card numbers. Carry one copy in a separate place to the originals and leave a copy with someone at home.

7. Check with health professionals for information on recommended **vaccinations**

or other **precautions** and find out about overseas laws on traveling with medicines.

8. Ensure your passport has at least six months' **validity** from your planned date of return. Some countries will refuse entry on arrival and some airlines will not allow passengers to board flights if their passport does not meet this requirement. Before traveling, you should contact the Embassy or High Commission of each country you intend to visit to confirm the entry requirements.

9. Leave a copy of your travel **itinerary** with someone at home and keep in regular contact with friends and relatives while overseas.

> destination [ˌdestɪˈneɪʃn] n. 目的地，终点
> subscribe [səbˈskraɪb] vi. (to) 订阅，订购
> notification [ˌnəʊtɪfɪˈkeɪʃn] n. 通知
> medical evacuation [ɪˌvækjuˈeɪʃn] n. 医疗救助
> participate [pɑːˈtɪsɪpeɪt] vi. 参加，参与
> embassy [ˈembəsɪ] n. 大使馆
> high commission 高级专员
> consulate [ˈkɒnsjʊlɪt] n. 领事馆
> emergency [ɪˈmɜːdʒənsɪ] n. 紧急情况，非常时刻
> override [ˌəʊvəˈraɪd] vt. 优先于
> harsh [hɑːʃ] adj. 严厉(酷)的
> transit [ˈtrænsɪt] n. 过境；通过，中转
> vaccination [ˌvæksɪˈneɪʃn] n. 疫苗接种
> precaution [prɪˈkɔːʃn] n. 预防
> validity [vəˈlɪdɪtɪ] n. 有效期
> itinerary [aɪˈtɪnərərɪ] n. 行程表，旅行路线
> dual [ˈdjuːəl] adj. 双(重)的

10. Before departing, check whether you are regarded as a national of the country you intend to visit. Research whether holding **dual** nationality has any implications for your travel.

 Reading A

Advantages and Disadvantages of Various Tours

Tours can be a convenient, affordable and relatively safe way to travel. Basically, tour operators can offer you the benefits of economies of scale, security and travel experience. They buy hotel rooms, air, ship and motor coach travel, rental car contracts, sightseeing tours, services and even restaurant meals **in bulk** so they can negotiate low cost deals. Buying in bulk, in advance, can sometimes give them **access to** travel arrangements and accommodations you might not be able to get any other way. Consider the advantages of tours in general and then look at the advantages and disadvantages of the different types before deciding which one is for you.

Escorted Tours

An escorted tour is the most traditional kind. It usually involves group travel with accommodation, activities and meals included. Generally, the tour will follow a set itinerary and will be accompanied by a tour director or guide. Sometimes local guides and experts may join in.

The advantages: Affordable travel; No language problems; Cover a lot of territory in a short time; Safety and security; Lots of traveling companions; Chance to learn from experts; Ease of travel in areas.

> in bulk 大量,大批
> access to 接近
> escorted tours 全程陪同旅游
> regimentation [ˌredʒɪmenˈteɪʃn] n. 严格控制
> superficial [ˌsuːpəˈfɪʃəl] adj. 肤浅的,表面的
> gear [ɡɪə] vt. (to)使适合
> denominator [dɪˈnɒmɪneɪtə] n. 平均水平
> get stuck with 无法摆脱,困于
> incompatible [ˌɪnkəmˈpætəbəl] adj. 不相容的

The disadvantages: **Regimentation**; Potential for **superficial** visits or for moving on too quickly to the next place; Lack of free time to rest or for independent exploring; Meals, sightseeing and information geared to the lowest common **denominator**; Chance you'll **get stuck with incompatible** traveling companions; No flexibility to change travel plans along the way.

What to look out for: What is included in the price? Does it include all entrance fees or are the interesting excursions extra? Do the meals include wines and alcoholic beverages? Will you have freedom to choose what you like from the menu? Is the tour operator a member of a reputable industry organization?

Package Tours

Package tours like escorted tours usually have fixed itineraries with hotels, and all transportation(including local transfers) booked and paid for in advance. The difference is, there is no group. Once you arrive, you are on your own to visit and see what you want. The tour operator may make a range of excursions and local transit arrangements available—at extra but reduced prices. And the operator will usually have a representative available at the destination to handle problems or book local outings.

The advantages: Economies of scale; Local assistance available; Freedom and flexibility within fixed destinations; Suggested excursions at reduced prices.

> package tour 包价旅行(由旅行社安排一切的一揽子旅游)
> penalty [ˈpenltɪ] n. 惩罚,罚款

The disadvantages: Main travel arrangements are fixed and inflexible; Hotels on the package tour routes can often be second-rate.

What to look out for: Do you have a choice of accommodation? What are the **penalties** for last minute travel changes? Is there a good choice of local excursions, meal and transit deals?

Self-guided Tours

Self-guided tours are a new and popular alternative for cycling, hiking and, to some degree, motoring vacations. There is no group and you are on your own but your itinerary is made in advance for you. Accommodations are arranged and paid for in advance, restaurants may be booked, and it is up to you to cycle, hike or drive to the next stop along the way. Maps, lists of useful local phone numbers and emergency services may be provided.

The advantages: Very independent and flexible; Tailored packages available; Suitable for couples, families or groups of friends; You tour at your own pace.

The disadvantages: May cost more than other kinds of tours; You need to be able to read maps; You may need some ability in the local language.

What to look out for: Can you tailor the time and distance between stops to suit your ability? Is key equipment provided or available to rent? What exactly is included in the price? Some self-guided tours may include restaurant meals and accommodation in the price while others may simply make the arrangements and leave local payment up to you. Are maps and other required information adequate and understandable?

Reading B

Tour on Holiday

universal [ˌjuːnɪˈvɜːsəl] adj. 普遍的
phenomena [fɪˈnɒmɪnə] n. (pl.) 现象
rigid [ˈrɪdʒɪd] adj. 严格的,死板的
compact [kəmˈpækt] adj. 紧凑的
linger [ˈlɪŋɡə] vi. 逗留,留恋徘徊
inhale [ɪnˈheɪl] v. 吸入(气体等)
budget [ˈbʌdʒɪt] n. 预算

It is one of the **universal phenomena** that more and more people choose to spend their holiday on tours. Before you start a tour, it is important to know which kind of tour suits you. Some people like package tour, because the travel agency will prepare everything for you, such as transportation, accommodation, meals, and the scenic spots to be visited. What you need to do is to take your camera and luggage, following the guide. It's really very convenient and easy. However, some people complain that in this kind of tour, the itinerary is **rigid** and **compact**. You are always urged by the guide from one place to another place and have almost no freedom to **linger** on the spots where you'd like to stay longer. Therefore, they prefer traveling on their own, for it

Unit 1 Giving Travel Information

is more flexible and relaxing. You can spend a whole day on the beach or in a forest, enjoying the sunshine or **inhaling** the fresh air. In spite of these differences of tours, the purpose of having a tour on holiday is the same, that is, to relax yourself and have fun. So if you can plan it well, you'll have more fun. The following things should be considered before you start:

- **budget**
- transportation
- accommodation
- meals
- the scenic spots to be visited

 **Speaking**

Dialogue A (A: staff, B: Smith)

A: Can I help you?

B: My wife and I want to go to Beijing for a tour. Can you arrange it?

A: Yes, we can arrange that.

B: I'd like to know what kind of tour your travel agency has.

A: Our travel agency provides all kinds of tours, ranging from individual tours to group package tours.

B: Excellent.

A: When do you expect to come?

B: July 28th.

A: What specific places do you wish to visit?

B: We would like to visit the Great Wall, the Summer Palace and the Imperial Palace.

A: OK.

Dialogue B (A: staff, B: Smith)

A: Good morning. What can I do for you?

B: Could you give me some information on your tours?

A: Of course, yes. Here you are.

B: I am interested in the two-day trip.

A: You are lucky. The tour is still available.

B: What is the cost?

A: The price for one person is 1,198 *yuan*.

B: That sounds reasonable. Can I make a reservation now?

A: Yes. Just a moment, please.

Dialogue C (A: Smith, B: staff)

A: Hi! I need some sightseeing advice.

B: That's what I'm here for, sir. Every good hotel has a staff like me.

A: I don't travel a lot. Would you please give me some information? And where should I go first?

B: I'd suggest that you start at the Shenyang Imperial Palace.

A: You know, I've already been there. Can you suggest another place?

B: Maybe. Tell me what you like to do in your spare time.

A: When I have some free time, I often spend it running or at museums.

B: Well, have you ever been to Qipanshan Mountain Park or the Museum of Liaoning?

A: No, but I sure would like to.

B: Qipanshan Mountain Park is great for just about everything outdoors. Then you can visit the Museum of Liaoning.

A: Both places sound great. I'll try to do that.

B: Enjoy the views at both places.

Dialogue D (A: Sam, B: staff)

A: Hi, is this where I can get information on tours?

B: Yes, I can help you with that. What type of tour are you thinking about? There are some great city tours that are half-day or full-day.

A: You know, we've explored the city a lot since we've been here. I was actually thinking of a side trip.

B: Oh, sure. We have excursions to nearby attractions. There are one-day trips or two-day overnight trips, depending on which one you pick.

A: I think I'm interested in a hiking trip to the mountains. I'm big on nature. Are the overnight trips expensive?

B: Not at all. They are very moderately priced, starting at RMB 120 *yuan* and up. Here's a brochure on the three hiking tours that are available. All three are guided tours, and meals and transportation are included.

A: Do I need to book ahead?

B: Yes, this company requires that you make a reservation 24 hours ahead.

A: Great. I'll take a look at the brochure. Can I book that here at the hotel tour desk, or do I call the company directly?

B: I can book that for you. Just stop by when you've made a decision and I'll take care

Unit 1 Giving Travel Information

of it for you.

A: That's great. Thanks a lot for your help.

B: It's my pleasure. Let me know if you have any questions.

A: I will. Thanks.

Functional Sentences

旅游咨询

* Where is the tourist information? 旅游咨询中心在哪里？
* Welcome to our travel agency. 欢迎来到我们旅行社。
* Can you give me more detail on what's included in the package? 能不能告诉我全部行程的细节？
* I have to think about it before I decide on a program. 在我选定旅游项目前,我得考虑考虑。
* Are all meals included in the price? 三餐都包含在费用之内吗？
* Is there any extra charge? 有没有其他额外费用？
* I'd like to have more information about your tour package to…
  我想了解一下你们到……去的旅游路线的具体情况。
* How many people will be in this tour? 有多少人参加这次旅行呢？
* We would like to visit some places of real Beijing ordinary life, could you recommend some packages?
  我们想要游览一些有真正北京民俗的地方,你们能推荐一些线路吗？
* If you choose this package we can offer you a 20% discount.
  如果您选择这条路线,我们可以给您打八折。
* What will this price include? 这个价格包含什么？

Exercises

一、Complete the following dialogues.

Dialogue 1 (A: guest, B: staff)

A: Hi, I was told to see you about going sightseeing.

B: _____. I'm the hotel's staff, at your service.

A: Very good. _____?

B: I would suggest the Imperial Palace.

A: Gee, I've already seen the Imperial Palace. What about another site?

B: Let me see. _____?

A: Well, I really like to run. And I like art.

B: Well, there you go! Have you ever visited either Qipanshan Mountain Park or the Museum of Liaoning?

A: No, _____.

B: Well, Qipanshan Mountain Park is fantastic for running. Then you can go to the Museum of Liaoning to look at the beautiful art.

A: _____. I'll do that.

B: Enjoy your run and your visit!

Dialogue 2 (A: guest, B: staff)

A: Hi! I need some sightseeing advice. I was told to come to see you.

B: As your concierge, _____, sir.

A: Concierge? Are we speaking English here?

B: A concierge helps you find all the great places for visiting, shopping, and eating.

A: Well, _____?

B: How about starting at the Forbidden City? Many people like to begin there.

A: The last time I was here, I visited the Forbidden City. _____?

B: I think so. _____.

A: I'm big on running, although maybe I like art even more than running.

B: Then you must go to Xiangshan Mountain Park and the Museum of China! Have you been to either one?

A: No. _____.

B: Both places are usually crowded with natives and tourists. You'll love the Park and the Museum.

A: Thank you. That's great advice.

B: This might be the best day of your visit.

二、Complete the dialogue with the Chinese prompts.

A: 能为您效劳吗?

B: 我和我妻子想去北京旅游。你们能安排吗?

A: 可以,我们可以安排。

B: 我想问一下你们旅行社都有一些什么样的旅游项目?

A: 我们旅行社提供各种旅游项目,从散客旅游到团队报价旅游都有。

B: 太好了。

A：你们打算什么时候来？

B：10月8号。

A：你们具体想参观哪些地方？

B：我们想参观长城、故宫、颐和园。

A：好的。

三、Put the following into English.

1. 旅游咨询中心在哪里？
2. 您能为我安排一次旅行吗？
3. 你准备怎么走？是乘火车还是乘飞机？
4. 三餐都包含在费用里吗？
5. 有没有其他的额外费用？
6. 我决定参加为期一周的泰国旅游团。
7. 您要申请什么样的签证？
8. 我能看一下您的返程机票吗？
9. 您持有的是旅游签证还是公务签证？
10. 签证准备好时我们会通知您。

四、Role play.

Student A：You are a guest. You come to a travel agency and ask the clerk whether there is a package tour on Beijing folk customs.

Student B：You are the clerk. You present him several package tours and the guest chooses one.

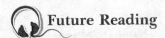

Spring Festival

The Spring Festival is the most important festival for the Chinese people and is when all family members get together, just like Christmas in the West. All people living away from home go back, becoming the busiest time for transportation systems of about half a month from the Spring Festival. Airports, railway stations and long-distance bus stations are crowded with home returnees.

The Spring Festival falls on the 1st day of the 1st lunar month, often one month later than the Gregorian calendar. It originated in the

Shang Dynasty (1600 BC—1046 BC) from the people's sacrifice to gods and ancestors at the end of an old year and the beginning of a new one.

Strictly speaking, the Spring Festival starts every year in the early days of the 12th lunar month and will last till the mid 1st lunar month of the next year. Of them, the most important days are Spring Festival Eve and the first three days. The Chinese government now stipulates people have seven days off for the Chinese Lunar New Year.

Spring Festival is the most important festival in China. It's to celebrate the lunar calendar's new year. In the evening before the Spring Festival, families get together and have a big meal. In many places people like to set off firecrackers. Dumplings are the most traditional food. Children like the festival very much, because they can have delicious food and wear new clothes. They can also get some money from their parents. This money is given to children for good luck. People put New Year scrolls on the wall for good fortune.

The Spring Festival lasts about 15 days long. People visit relatives and friends with the words "Have all your wishes". People enjoy the Spring Festival, during this time they can have a good rest.

Probably more food is consumed during the New Year celebrations than any other time of the year. Vast amounts of traditional food is prepared for family and friends, as well as those close to us who have died.

On New Year's Day, the Chinese family will eat a vegetarian dish called jai. Although the various ingredients in jai are root vegetables or fibrous vegetables, many people attribute various superstitious aspects to them.

Other foods include a whole fish, to represent togetherness and abundance, and a chicken for prosperity. The chicken must be presented with a head, tail and feet to symbolize completeness. Noodles should be uncut, as they represent long life.

In south China, the favorite and most typical dishes were nian gao, sweet steamed glutinous rice(糯米)pudding and zongzi [glutinous rice wrapped up in reed(芦苇) leaves], another popular delicacy.

In the north, steamed-wheat bread (man tou) and small meat dumplings were the preferred food. The tremendous amount of food prepared at this time was meant to symbolize abundance and wealth for the household.

Unit 2　At the Airport

Unit Objectives

Master the basic words and expressions about the airport;

Get some background knowledge about meeting a tour group at the airport;

Know some cultural knowledge of checking procedures for the international passengers.

Background Knowledge

Tips for Meeting a Tour Group at the Airport

1. Make sure the arrival time of the tourists' flight before going to receive the tourists.

2. Contact the bus driver, and inform him of the starting time and meeting place. Be sure to get to the destination half an hour earlier.

3. Arrive at the destination half an hour earlier, talk with the driver over the best parking place. Then contact the information desk of the airport, **verify** the exact time of tourist's arrival.

4. Before meeting the tour group, inform the baggage clerk where and when to fetch baggage and where to send the baggage.

5. Before the tour group comes out, stand at a **visible** place where passengers exit, with receiving sign held high in the hand. On the sign,

> verify ['verɪfaɪ] vt. 核实,查对
> visible ['vɪzəbl] adj. 看得见的,明显的

there should be the name of the tour group, the number of the group, and the name of the tour leader.

Reading A

Meeting tourists is just the first step in the whole working **procedure** of a tour guide. As a guide, you should bear in your mind the following things: Firstly, try to get the right tour group you are supposed to meet, pay attention to characteristics of different nationalities and the **logo** of their foreign tour groups.

procedure [prəˈsiːdʒə] n. 程序,手续,步骤
logo [ˈləʊɡəʊ] n. (企业、公司等的)专用标识
domestic [dəˈmestɪk] adj. 国内的
depart [dɪˈpɑːt] vi. 离开,出发
regulation [ˌreɡjuˈleɪʃn] n. 规章,规则
comply [kəmˈplaɪ] vi. (with)遵从,依从,服从
customs [ˈkʌstəmz] adj. 海关的
embarkation [ˌembɑːˈkeɪʃn] n. 乘船,搭机
currency [ˈkʌrənsi] n. 货币
diplomat [ˈdɪpləmæt] n. 外交官,外交家

In most countries, the **domestic** passenger comes to the airport, shows his ticket at the airline counter, checks in his baggage and his flight. Upon arrival at his destination, he picks up his baggage and goes on his way.

The international passenger, on the other hand, goes through a much more complicated process. For the **departing** passenger, there may be government **regulations** with which to **comply** in addition to the airline check-in process. For the arriving passenger, there are always passport and **customs** procedures. For the international passenger, there is even a special category—the transit passenger who is stopping at an airport that is not his destination. Because of the special problems of international passengers, this will summarize the procedures that apply to them on most airlines and at most airports around the world.

Procedures for the departing international passenger are usually quite simple, though they may vary considerably from country to country. In most countries, the passenger completes the airline check-in and then goes through some form of passport control. He will probably be required to fill out an **embarkation** card, which will be kept by passport officials or police. From the passport-issued countries, the passenger cannot be accompanied into the departure area, and a few countries may also require some sort of **currency** or baggage check for outgoing passengers. But the later is unusual.

Passenger service agents at the airport must be thoroughly familiar with the government procedures through which the passenger is required to pass. The agents must know, for example, whether there will be checks other than passport control or whether passengers who require special treatment, such as VIPS, **diplomats**, people with language problems, and so on.

Reading B

Questions are asked at the Customs

When you travel abroad, you must first pass through Customs after getting off the plane. The Custom officers may ask you some questions. Then what questions will be asked by the Custom officers? For example, what's the purpose of your visit? What's in your bag? And you also need to fill in a **Customs declaration form**. The followings are often asked by the Custom officers.

Customs declaration form 海关申报表
souvenir [ˌsuːvəˈnɪə] n. 纪念品,纪念物
duty [ˈdjuːtɪ] n. 税;关税

Officer: May I see your passport, please?

Henry: Sure. Here you are. May I have a Customs declaration form, please?

Officer: OK. Here you are.

Henry: Could you explain how to fill this out?

Officer: Do you have anything to declare?

Henry: I have nothing to declare.

Officer: What's the purpose of your visit?

Henry: I'm here on business.

Officer: This visa is good for two weeks. How long will you be staying?

Henry: For ten days.

Officer: Please open this bag. What are these?

Henry: These are for my personal use. These are gifts for my friends. This is a **souvenir** that I'm taking to Beijing.

Officer: Do you have any liquor or cigarettes?

Henry: Yes, I have two bottles of whisky. And this camera is for my personal use.

Officer: You'll have to pay **duty** on this. Do you have any other baggage?

Henry: Yes. Just clothes, and some books.

Officer: And you will do some traveling while you are here?

Henry: Yes. I want to spend a couple of days for traveling. I have friends there I will visit.

Officer: OK. Enjoy your trip, sir.

Henry: Thank you.

Speaking

New Words & Phrases

scale [skeɪl] *n.* 磅秤

claim baggage 提取行李

Dialogue A (A: tour guide, B: guest)

A: Excuse me! Are you Mr. Green from Los Angeles?

B: Yes, I'm James Green.

A: Nice to meet you, Mr. Green. I'm Meng Li, your tour guide from the Youth Travel Service. Just call me Xiao Meng.

B: Nice to meet you, too.

A: (Meng Li shakes hands with Mr. Green and other guests) Welcome to China!

B: We're so glad you've come to meet us at the airport, Xiao Meng.

A: Did you have a good trip, Mr. Green?

B: Yes, quite pleasant. But we feel a bit tired after the long flight.

A: Yes, you must. You all need a good rest first.

B: Nevertheless we are all excited that we've finally arrived in the country that we have been wishing to see for years.

A: You will have plenty of time to see all the interesting places in China. Is everyone in the group here?

B: Yes, a party of ten. We have five ladies and five gentlemen.

A: Good. Can we go now? Shall I help you with your luggage, Mr. Green?

B: No, thanks. I can manage.

A: Please follow me, ladies and gentlemen! The shuttle bus is just waiting in the parking lot.

B: That's fine. Hurry up, guys!

A: This way, please.

Dialogue B (A: clerk, B: guest)

A: May I help you?

B: I'd like to check in for this flight.

A: Please put your luggage on this **scale**. You need to **claim your baggage** at the counter.

B: Can I take this one as carry-on baggage?

A: Sorry, you cannot.

B: Is the plane on schedule?

A: Sorry, I'm not sure.

B: Could I get a window seat?

A: Yes, of course.

B: What is the gate number?

A: You will be boarding at Gate 5.

B: I am taking economy class/business class/first class.

A: Thanks for your patience.

Dialogue C (A: clerk, B: guest)

A: Good afternoon. May I help you?

B: Yes. I'd like to check in, please.

A: May I see your ticket and passport, please?

B: Sure. Here they are.

A: Please put your baggage on the scale.

B: What's the weight limit?

A: Thirty two kilos.

B: I hope my baggage isn't overweight.

A: No, they aren't.

B: May I carry this baggage?

A: Sure. But please attach this claim tag.

B: OK.

A: Here is your boarding pass.

B: Which gate?

A: Gate Four. Please go and have a seat in the waiting hall.

B: Thank you.

Dialogue D (A: Mr. Li, B: Clerk in the information counter)

A: Do you have any direct flight to New Zealand?

B: Sorry, we don't. But I think you can fly on Northwest 212 to Tokyo and then have a connecting flight on Japan Airline 123 to Auckland. And it is the most economical flight, just USD 580.

A: When does the Flight 212 depart?

B: At 11:30 am. By the way, it also makes a refueling stop at Chicago.

A: How big is the layover at Chicago?

B: Less than one hour.

A: And how long do I have to stay in Tokyo for the connecting flight?

B: Not so long, just one hour.

A: So the time for the whole journey is about…

B: About eleven hours.

A: Let me count… OK, it works out for my time schedule. Thanks a lot.

B: You are welcome.

Dialogue E (A: staff, B: passenger)

A: Hello. This is South Airline.

B: I'd like to reconfirm my flight.

A: What's your name and flight number?

B: My name is Jerry Cheng, and the flight number is UA 003 for Los Angeles.

A: When is it?

B: June 10th. I'd like to make sure of the time it leaves.

A: I can't find your name.

B: Really?

A: May I have your name again? I still can't find your name on the reservation list. Anyway, we have seats for new bookings on this flight. No problem. One economy class seat, is that right? Now you have been booked.

B: Thanks a lot. What time do you start check-in?

A: Two hours before departure time. You must checkin at least one hour before.

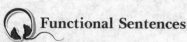 Functional Sentences

 机场接机

* Welcome to China!
  欢迎您到中国来!
* Did you have a good trip?
  旅行愉快吗?
* You all need a good rest first.
  你们都需要先休息一下。

* You will have plenty of time to see all the interesting places in China.
  你们会有很多时间欣赏中国的著名景点。
* Is everyone in the group here?
  全团的人都在吗?
* Shall I help you with your luggage?
  让我来帮您拿行李好吗?
* The shuttle bus is just waiting in the parking lot.
  大巴正在停车场等各位。

登机检查

* May I have your ticket and passport, please? 请出示您的机票和护照?
* Here are your ticket and passport, and here are your boarding pass and baggage checks. 这是您的机票和护照,这是您的登机牌和行李牌。
* Please show your passport at the counter. 请到柜台出示您的护照。
* Which is the security check counter? 哪个是安全检查的柜台?
* Here is my ticket. 这是我的机票。
* Please go upstairs and proceed through security check and immigration. 请上楼通过安全检查并办理出境手续。
* I have to check your bag before you go on board.
  在您登机前我得检查一下您的包。

检查行李

* Do you have any baggage to check in? 您有行李要托运吗?
* I have a bag to check in. 我有件行李要办托运。
* Where is the cheek-in counter? 托运行李的柜台在哪?
* Please put your two pieces of baggage on the conveyer belt one by one. 请您把两件行李一件一件地放在传送带上。
* These are your baggage checks. 这些是您的行李提单。
* Please put the baggage on the scale. 请把行李放到磅秤上。
* What should I do with my checked luggage? 我应该怎样处理我已托运的行李?

问题解答

* Where is Gate 5? 5号登机口在哪里？
* Tell me the gate number, please. 请告诉我登机口号码。
* When will the flight begin boarding? 航班什么时候开始登机？
* How much hand luggage am I allowed? 我可以携带多少件手提行李呢？
* Is this the line for the flight to Shanghai at 2:10 pm? 下午2点10分飞往上海的航班是在这里排队吗？
* Where should I go after checking in? 办完登机手续后我应往哪里走？
* Hand baggage is not to be weighed. 手提行李不用过秤。
* Could you show me how to fill in the declaration card? 您可以告诉我怎样填写申报表吗？
* Boarding is delayed. 登机推迟了。

 **Exercises**

一、**Complete the following dialogue.**

A: Hi. Is this the right counter to check in for CA588?

B: _____. May I have your ticket and passport, please?

A: _____.

B: How many pieces of luggage do you have?

A: Only one.

B: Please put your luggage on this scale.

A: OK. _____?

B: Yes, Miss. The flight will depart on time in an hour. Please proceed to Gate 10 and enjoy your trip.

二、**Complete the dialogues with the Chinese prompts.**

Dialogue 1

A: 早上好，请出示您的机票和护照。

B: 给您。

A: 您有行李要托运吗？

B: 是的，有一个箱子。

A: 请您把箱子放在磅秤上，好吗？

B: 好的。顺便问一下，您能告诉我每位乘客的免费行李额是多少吗？

A：免费行李额根据您所乘坐的舱位不同而不同。您坐的是什么舱位？

B：头等舱。

A：头等舱的旅客免费行李额为 40 千克。

B：我可以带几件行李上飞机呢？

A：持头等舱客票的旅客可以带两件总重量不超过 5 千克的行李上飞机。

B：如果我的行李超过限量怎样办呢？

A：如果您的托运行李超过限额,您得付超重行李费。

B：我明白了。谢谢您提供的信息。

A：别客气,您的登机牌和行李票。

B：再见。

Dialogue 2

A：您好,请问到市内最方便的方式是什么？

B：有几个方式。你可以乘坐城市公交,那是最便宜的。还有区间巴士和豪华大轿车 (limousines),但最快的方式是乘出租车。

A：好吧,我乘区间巴士。能告诉我在哪可以乘坐？

B：就在大门口。

Dialogue 3

A：你好,请问行李提领区在哪？

B：顺着这条道走到头,然后右拐。

A：谢谢。我如何知道在哪里提取我的行李？

B：你刚才乘坐的是哪个航班？

A：我乘美国联合航空公司 446 航班从东京来。

B：你会发现你的行李在三号传送带(carousel)上。

三、**Put the following into English.**

1. 欢迎您到中国来！
2. 你们都需要先休息一下。
3. 你们会有很多时间欣赏中国的著名景点。
4. 让我来帮您拿行李好吗？
5. 请出示您的机票和护照。
6. 哪个是安全检查的柜台？
7. 5 号登机口在哪里？
8. 航班什么时候开始登机？
9. 我可以携带多少件手提行李呢？
10. 您可以告诉我怎样填写申报表吗？

四、Role play.

Student A: You are the local guide from China International Travel Agency. You are at the airport to meet a travel group from USA. Mr. Smith is the group leader.

Student B: You are Mr. Smith. You meet the local guide at the airport. Now you are having a talk with the guide.

Future Reading

Tomb Sweeping Day (Qingming Festival)

The Qingming (Pure Brightness) Festival is one of the 24 seasonal division points in China, falling on April 4-6 each year. After the festival, the temperature will rise up and rainfall increases. It is the high time for spring plowing and sowing. But the Qingming Festival is not only a seasonal point to guide farm work, it is more a festival of commemoration.

The Qingming Festival sees a combination of sadness and happiness. This is the most important day of sacrifice. Both the Han and minority ethnic groups at this time offer sacrifices to their ancestors and sweep the tombs of the deceased. Also, they will not cook on this day and only cold food is served.

The Hanshi (Cold Food) Festival was usually one day before the Qingming Festival. As our ancestors often extended the day to the Qingming, they were later combined.

On each Qingming Festival, all cemeteries are crowded with people who came to sweep tombs and offer sacrifices. Traffic on the way to the cemeteries becomes extremely jammed. The customs have been greatly simplified today. After slightly sweeping the tombs, people offer food, flowers and favourites of the dead, then burn incense and paper money and bow before the memorial tablet.

In contrast to the sadness of the tomb sweepers, people also enjoy hope of spring on this day. The Qingming Festival is a time when the sun shines brightly, the trees and grass become green and nature is again lively. Since ancient times, people have followed the custom of spring outings. At this time tourists are everywhere.

People love to fly kites during the Qingming Festival. Kite flying is actually not limited to the Qingming Festival. Its uniqueness lies in that people fly kites not during the day, but also at night. A string of little lanterns tied onto the kite or the thread look like shining stars, and therefore, are called "god's lanterns".

The Qingming Festival is also a time to plant trees, for the survival rate of saplings is high and trees grow fast later. In the past, the Qingming Festival was called "Arbor Day". But since 1979, "Arbor Day" was settled on March 12 according to the Gregorian calendar.

Unit 3 Local Tour Guide Service

Unit Objectives

Master the basic words and expressions about local tour guide service;
Get some cultural knowledge of Shenyang and Beijing;
Know the qualities of a tour guide should have.

Background Knowledge

Qualities of a Tour Guide

A guide is the **representative** of a travel service and is often the only one that tour members will meet, then how to be a qualified guide.

1. Guides should have the **professional** knowledge.

In the work of tourism, professional knowledge is **vitally** important. In order to satisfy customers, you need to communicate, organize and arrange them, it is not easy, so you must have professional knowledge, if not, you can't deal with such things. As we know, knowledge is a base of everything, and you should understand the laws of developments of the things before handling them.

> representative [ˌreprɪˈzentətɪv] n. 代表
> professional [prəˈfeʃənl] adj. 职业的,专业的
> vitally [ˈvaɪtəli] adv. 极其重要地
> emotional [ɪˈməʊʃnəl] adj. 令人动情的;易动感情的
> proficient [prəˈfɪʃənt] adj. 熟练的,精通的
> archeology [ˌɑːkɪˈɒlədʒi] n. 考古学,古物
> architecture [ˈɑːkɪtektʃə] n. 建筑学(术、业)
> folklore [ˈfəʊklɔː] n. 民俗学,民间传说

2. Guides should have superb communication skills.

Guides should have a high-level language, be responsible for the guided tour of the customs of the region, and be clear to understand the **emotional** visitors. If they get it right, tour guides and visitors will be closer. If they have the same hearts, all the difficulties will become easier to solve.

3. Guides should be **proficient** in foreign languages.

4. Guides should have a broad range of cultural knowledge.

Different tourists have different needs of cultural knowledge, such as magnificent wars, flowers and birds, literature, **archeology**, arts, religions, medicine, **architecture**, gardens, **folklore**, clothes, food, weapons, entertainment, and so on.

5. Guides should be energetic and enthusiastic.

When applying for an American tour, the American wrote his personal qualities: energetic and warm; can deal with various personalities and all ages; has the ability to **resolve conflicts**; mild; have a sense of humor. In addition, guides should have at least the following basic conditions: healthy, clean, polite, **passionate**, smiling, **courageous**, **persevering**, hard-working, cheerful, and modest.

A tour guide should be able to act as an attendant, publicity agent, investigator and defender while accompanying foreign visitors. So, he or she has to have a perfect mastery of our Party's policies and political **ideology**, foreign language and knowledge. He or she must be honest and **upright**, free from **corruption**, **prudent** and careful in his or her work, **diligent** in his or her working style.

resolve [rɪˈzɒlv] vt. 解决(答)
conflict [ˈkɒnflɪkt] n. 冲突,争论
mild [maɪld] adj. 温和的,温柔的
passionate [ˈpæʃənɪt] adj. 充满激情的
courageous [kəˈreɪdʒəs] adj. 勇敢的;无畏的
persevering [ˌpɜːsɪˈvɪərɪŋ] adj. 坚忍不拔的
ideology [ˌaɪdɪˈɒlədʒɪ] n. 思想(体系),思想意识
upright [ˈʌpraɪt] adj. 正直的
corruption [kəˈrʌpʃən] n. 腐化,贪污
prudent [ˈpruːdənt] adj. 审慎的,小心谨慎的
diligent [ˈdɪlɪdʒənt] adj. 勤勉的,勤奋的

 Reading A

A Welcome Speech

Key points for a welcome speech.

- On behalf of the travel agency, the driver and you welcome the tourists.
- Tell the tourists your name, your mobile phone number and your travel service.
- Introduce the driver.
- Express your sincere desire to serve the tourists.
- Wish the tourists a good journey.

Good morning, ladies and gentlemen!

Welcome to Shenyang! We are leaving the airport for Kempinski Hotel in Shenyang where you will stay tonight. Now we are on our way to the hotel. Please sit back and relax. Your luggage will be sent to the hotel by another coach, so you don't have to worry about it.

First, let me introduce my colleague. This is Mr. Wang, our driver. He has more than 10 years of driving experience. My name is Zhanghua, and my English name is Carol. You can just call me Carol or Xiao Zhang. We are from Shenyang ABC International Travel Agency. On behalf of our travel agency, my colleague, I'd like to extend a warm-hearted welcome to all of you. During your stay in Shenyang, I will be your local guide. We'll try our best to make your visit go smoothly. If you have any problems, please don't hesitate to tell us. My mobile phone number is 13902406666. I'll have it switched on for 24 hours. Don't hesitate to contact me whenever you need to.

Now, we are on the way to our hotel. It is a five-star hotel in the downtown areas of Shenyang. Look out of the windows! We are driving across the famous Hunhe River,

> magnificent [mæg'nɪfɪsənt] adj. 壮丽的,宏伟的
> thrive [θraɪv] vi. 兴旺,繁荣
> ratify ['rætɪfaɪ] vt. 正式批准
> feast [fiːst] v. 款待,享受

which is a mother river in Shenyang and Fushun. From the bridge, you can see the rolling water running to west with some boats going back and forth on it. Attention, there is a **magnificent** building setting beside the river. It is Olympic Sports Centre which presents **thriving** of Shenyang.

Ladies and gentlemen! Shenyang is a city with a long history and bright culture. It is one of the famous historical and cultural cities **ratified** by the State Council. You will **feast** your eyes on both culture sites and natural sites. The famous scenic spots you are going to visit include the Imperial Palace, the Beiling Park, the Qipanshan Scenic Spots, just to name a few. Shenyang has many famous food, like Laobian Jiaozi, Xiongzhou Beef Jerky, Bulaolin Sweets. Shenyang also has some famous streets which are best places for you to go shopping, such as Zhongjie Street, Taiyuanjie Street, and Beihang Street. Now we are arriving at the Liaoning Broadcasting and Television Tower, 305.5 meters high, which is the highest building in the northeast of China.

As a Chinese old saying goes, "Isn't it delightful to meet friends from a far?" I am very happy to see you from Europe and I shall do my best to make your trip pleasant. Today we will hold a welcome party for you. I hope you will enjoy the wonderful Shenyang snacks. At the party, I will tell you the itinerary of your tour in Shenyang.

Oh, we have arrived at the Kempinski Hotel. Now please get off one by one, and follow me to check in.

Reading B

Beijing

Beijing is the nation's political, economic, cultural and educational center as well as China's most important center for international trade and communications. Beijing is one of the six ancient cities in China. It has been the heart and soul of politics and society throughout its long history and consequently there is an **unparalleled** wealth of discovery to delight and **intrigue** travelers as they explore Beijing's ancient past and enjoy its exciting modern development.

> unparalleled [ʌnˈpærəleld] adj. 无比的
> intrigue [ɪnˈtriːɡ] vt. 激起兴趣，迷住
> abundance [əˈbʌndəns] n. 大量，丰富，充足

Beijing is a city with four distinct seasons. Its best is late spring and autumn. But autumn is taken as the golden tourist season of the year since there is sometimes in the spring of recent years, a yellow wind. We suggest tourists visit Beijing during the months of May, September, and October when people can enjoy bright sunshine and blue skies. An **abundance** of international class performances are presented in May. If you like winter, you will have other chances to appreciate another landscape of Beijing. After skiing in Beihai Park and viewing the snowy sights on West Hill, enjoying the steaming hotpot is the best choice, which is really the fun of tour in Beijing. Please keep warm and remember to bring your **down garments** and sweaters when you visit Beijing in the winter.

Although now Beijing is a modern and fashionable city complete with a full 21st Century **vitality**, you can experience **authentic** Beijing life and become **acquainted** with old Beijing by exploring its many teahouses, temple fairs, Beijing's Hutong and Courtyard and enjoy the Peking Opera. Add any or all of these to your Beijing tour and

> down garment 羽绒服
> vitality [vaɪˈtælɪti] n. 活力；生命力
> authentic [ɔːˈθentɪk] adj. 真的，真正的
> acquainted [əˈkweɪntɪd] adj. 熟悉的，认识的
> matchless [ˈmætʃləs] adj. 无敌的，无比的
> vigor [ˈvɪɡə] n. 活力
> acrobatics [ˌækrəˈbætɪks] n. 杂技
> martial [ˈmɑːʃəl] adj. 军事的；战争的
> enchantment [ɪnˈtʃɑːntmənt] n. 着魔，喜悦
> encounter [ɪnˈkaʊntə] vt. 遇到

you will leave with a feeling of special appreciation in your heart for this ancient city that has truly seen it all and tells its story with **matchless** grace, charm and **vigor**.

After a day's Beijing tour, nighttime can hold other surprises for you. These can vary from traditional performances such as the Peking Opera, **acrobatics** and **martial arts** to modern ones including concerts, ballroom dancing, pubs and clubs. Each and every one has its individual **enchantment** for the tourist. No description of our capital city is complete without mention of the friendly people. Everywhere you will **encounter** smiling faces and a warm welcome, especially from the children who love to say 'Hello'. All these things add up to truly make your visit a cultural experience of a lifetime.

Speaking

New Words & Phrases

meditate ['medɪteɪt] *vi.* 沉思

precaution [prɪ'kɔːʃn] *n.* 预防,防备,警惕

pickpocket ['pɪkpɒkɪt] *n.* 扒手

instinct ['ɪnstɪŋkt] *n.* 本能,直觉;生性,天性

charity ['tʃærɪtɪ] *n.* [*pl.*] 慈善团体

street vendor 街头小贩

gorgeous ['ɡɔːdʒəs] *adj.* 华丽的;灿烂的

bund [bʌnd] *n.* 外滩

explicit [ɪk'splɪsɪt] *adj.* 详尽的;明确的;清楚的

cruise [kruːz] *v.* 巡游;巡航

Dialogue A (A: staff, B: guest)

A: Yes, sir. May I help you?

B: I'm interested in a tour.

A: Is there anything special you want to see?

B: Yes, I'm interested in seeing the Imperial Palace and the Beiling Park.

A: All right. Let me give you some brochures. We have three basic tours.

B: Does the morning tour visit the Imperial Palace and the Beiling Park?

A: No, sir. That's in the all-day tour.

B: Then, I'd better take the all-day tour.

A: That's a tour of all the most famous places.

B: Where do I meet the bus?

A: At the gate of Kempinski Hotel at nine thirty.

B: Fine. Please reserve me a seat for this Saturday. How long is the tour?

A: It takes six hours, sir.

B: I see. Can I pay in traveler's checks?

A: Of course. That's fifty, sir.

Dialogue B (A: visitor 1, B: visitor 2)

A: This is really a fascinating city!

B: Yes. This city is thousands of years old and has quite a history!

A: I really love this temple we are visiting.

B: As you enter the temple, please remove your shoes as the others are doing.

A: It is so quiet here.

B: Yes. They are showing respect to their gods. People come here to pray and **meditate**.

A: I noticed that the women all have some sort of head covering.

B: It is a tradition that women cover their heads while in the temple.

A: I noticed that all of the people were eating with their hands at dinner last night.

B: Yes. That is another custom that people practice here.

Dialogue C (A: guest, B: staff)

A: Do I need to take any special safety **precautions** in this city?

B: This is a very large city with a lot of crowds to work your way through. Keep in mind that poverty makes people a little more desperate.

A: What should I watch out for?

B: You have to pay special attention at train stations, airports, and tourist sites. They are known for having a lot of **pickpockets**.

A: There are so many children begging on the street that I don't know which one to give money to.

B: It is a natural **instinct** to want to give money to those children, but it is better to give money to one of the local **charities** or schools.

A: Are the local food and drink safe?

B: Avoid eating food prepared by **street vendors**. Use only bottled water.

A: How safe is it to be out at night?

B: You should always travel with others at night and stick to well-lit areas.

Dialogue D (A: tourist, B: guide)

A: This is my first trip to Shanghai, but I heard a long time ago that Shanghai was "Oriental Manhattan", and it looks like that fame is well deserved.

B: Wow, your Chinese is so good!

A: You're too kind. Hey, these houses are really pretty! They don't look like Chinese buildings.

B: Many people say so. These buildings have different European architectural styles. They are known as the "Exhibition of World Architectures".

A: They're **gorgeous** and in harmony with each other. Who built these buildings?

B: In the past, many foreign countries set up their consulates in this area. And the **Bund** also gathered the headquarters of international financial institutions in China.

A: What's that? Is it the famous Bund?

B: Yes, you're quite right. Here we are at the Bund, the most famous sightseeing spot in Shanghai. The place we are standing now is the newly built flood-prevention wall. Do you know what is it used to be?

A: We have no idea.

B: Here used to be a shabby chest-high brick wall called the "Lovers' Wall" along the Huangpu River. The meaning is quite **explicit**, I think.

A: What a romantic place it was!

B: But the newly-built sightseers' wall is wider than ever and one can enjoy a broader sight. Please turn your eyes across the river. Can you see the tower with bright "pearls"?

A: Yes. Is that the TV tower? What's the name of it?

B: The Oriental Pearl TV Tower. People say it's like a bright pearl on the Huangpu River. It is 450 meters high and boasts the tallest in Asia, and is a new attraction in Shanghai.

A: What a sight the Bund is!

B: You can say that again! Now, ladies and gentlemen, time for us to go on a **cruise** on the Huangpu River. Please on board, everybody!

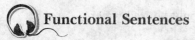 Functional Sentences

 饭店途中

* Is everybody on the bus? 每个人都在车上了吗?

* Shall we go now? 我们现在可以出发了吗?
* Let me introduce my team to you first. 首先让我来向大家介绍一下我的团队。
* We will do our best to make your trip more enjoyable and memorable.
  我们将尽最大努力使你们的旅行更有趣、更难忘。
* It's one of the best five-star hotels in the city.
  它是这个城市最好的五星级酒店之一。
* I hope you will enjoy your stay there. 我希望你能在那住得愉快。
* Next, I'd like to introduce something about this city.
  接下来,我想要介绍一下有关这个城市的一些情况。
* There're many famous scenic spots and historical sites in Shenyang.
  在沈阳有很多著名的景点和名胜古迹。

本地参团

* I would like to join your tours to Shanghai on September 10th.
  我想参加你们 9 月 10 号去上海的旅游团。
* Do we have a guide who can speak English? 我们会有英语导游吗?
* How many people will join this tour? 有多少人要报名参加这个团?
* Can I have the details of the schedule of this tour?
  我能详细了解一下这条线路的安排吗?
* Do you have any special requirements? 您还有什么特殊要求吗?
* We would like to take a double room with a front view.
  我们想要住一间阳面的双人房。
* Can we have our tour extended? 我们的旅行能延长一段时间吗?
* Where can I have my traveler's check cashed? 我在哪里可以兑换旅行支票啊?
* Do I have to buy the insurance additionally? 我还需要额外购买保险吗?
* Insurance is included in the package fee. 您交的费用中已经包含保险了。
* My wife has some motion sickness, so can the local guide prepare some medicine in case of emergency?
  我妻子有些晕车,地陪导游可以准备一些晕车药以备不时之需吗?

Exercises

一、Complete the following dialogue.

A: I was wondering if you could help me book a few tours.

B: You have come to the right place. _____?

A: I will be here for a week.

B: _____?

A: This is my first time visiting this city.

B: What are you interested in? Do you enjoy museums and buildings, or would you rather hit some outdoor hotspots and venues?

A: _____.

B: We have tours for all interests.

A: Do you have a city tour?

B: Yes, in fact, I usually suggest that to visitors.

二、Complete the dialogues with the Chinese prompts.

Dialogue 1

A：今天我们应该到哪里去观光呢？

B：我想有些东西最好在上午做，其他的下午完成。

A：我想上午去海滩。

B：那是开始我们旅游观光的很好的地方。我们可以在那吃早餐。

A：我听说那有一个非常好的自然历史博物馆。

B：是的，去那看看很好，因为我们离那很近。

A：下午我们去哪呢？

B：我想去游乐场。那可能是个好地方。

A：一天结束的时候，我想在公园附近的餐厅看日落。

B：是个好主意。咱们去买个地图吧。

Dialogue 2

A：打扰了，请问门票多少钱？

B：周末是免费的。

A：太好啦！

B：这是导游图。

A：谢谢。顺便问一下，我能在公园里拍照吗？

B：是的，为什么不能？

A：那公园里有商店吗？

B：是的，有好多商店，你几乎可以在那买到任何东西。

A：我知道了。十分感谢。

B：不用客气。

三、Put the following into English.

1. 我想参加你们 7 月 10 号去上海的旅游团。
2. 我们会有英语导游吗？
3. 我能详细了解一下这条线路的安排吗？
4. 我们想要住一间阳面的双人房。
5. 在沈阳有很多著名的景点和名胜古迹。
6. 我们将尽最大努力使你们的旅行更有趣、更难忘。
7. 接下来，我想要介绍一下有关这个城市的一些情况。
8. 您交的费用中已经包含保险了。
9. 我妻子有些晕车，地陪导游可以准备一些晕车药以备不时之需吗？
10. 首先让我来向大家介绍一下我的团队。

四、Role play.

Suppose you are now showing your foreign tourists around your hometown and you are telling them something about the famous scenic spots and the traditional Chinese culture in your hometown.

Dragon Boat Festival

The Dragon Boat Festival, also called the Duanwu Festival, is celebrated on the fifth day of the fifth month according to the Chinese calendar. For thousands of years, the festival has been marked by eating zong zi (glutinous rice wrapped to form a pyramid using bamboo or reed leaves) and racing dragon boats.

The festival is best known for its dragon-boat races, especially in the southern provinces where there are many rivers and lakes. This regatta commemorates the death of Qu Yuan, an honest minister who is said to have committed suicide by drowning himself in a river.

The people of Chu who mourned the death of Qu threw rice into the river to feed his ghost every year on the fifth day of the fifth month. But one year, the spirit of Qu appeared and told the mourners that a huge reptile in the river had stolen the rice. The spirit then advised them to wrap the rice in silk and bind it with five different-colored threads before tossing it into the river.

During the Duanwu Festival, a glutinous rice pudding called zong zi is eaten to symbolize the rice offerings to Qu. Ingredients such as beans, lotus seeds, chestnuts, pork fat and the golden yolk of a salted duck egg are often added to the glutinous rice. The pudding is then wrapped with bamboo leaves, bound with a kind of raffia and boiled in salt water for hours.

Unit 4　Shopping

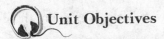

Master the basic words and expressions about shopping in traveling;
Get some cultural knowledge about shopping in China;
Get some information about shopping malls.

Background Knowledge

How to Bargain in China

It is very common that when Chinese sellers see foreign buyers, they will definitely offer high price. So it is necessary to do some **bargaining**, there are some tips which may be helpful to you:

> bargain ['bɑːgən] vi. 讨价还价
> porcelain ['pɔːsəlɪn] n. 瓷器

1. Deciding how low to begin your side of the bargaining depends on what you're shopping for. For the inexpensive stuffs, For example, a **porcelain** tea cup should probably be about RMB 25 (US＄3). If the seller asks for RMB 50, you can offer 15rmb and work up from there. And it's better to start lower than your target price.

2. Take your time and don't be rush. If the vendor is not willing to low down the price, take a walk around and you probably find the cheaper one elsewhere.

3. Don't feel sorry for the vendor if you don't want to buy. Some vendors may be not happy if you do not buy anything from them after some time visiting, so just respond to them politely and walk away from the shops. You have your own right to

decide what you want to buy or not.

4. Use the walk-away method, this is very workable sometimes.

Reading A

| essential [ɪˈsenʃ(ə)l] adj. 必需的；基本的 |
| necessity [nəˈsesətɪ] n. 必需品 |
| preserve [prɪˈzɜːv] vi. 做蜜饯，做果酱，做罐头 |
| handicraft [ˈhændɪkrɑːft] n. 手工艺品 |
| commodity [kəˈmɒdɪtɪ] n. [pl.]日用品；商品 |

Shopping is one of the **essential** factors of tourism. Wherever they go, travelers will buy daily **necessities**. They will also buy many things needed during a tour, for example, a camera, travel bags, tourist maps and drinks. Tourists are always ready to buy special products of local places. Take for instance, people tend to buy porcelain in Jingde Town of Jiangxi Province, **preserved** fruits in Beijing and so on. The **handicraft**s stores and souvenir shops are favorite places for tourists to visit. In fact, people always carry some money for shopping during their tour.

Conditions for shopping—shopping environment and the abundance of goods can directly affect the development of tourism industry of a place. Shopping is actually an attraction for tourists. It is especially true for large modern cities such as London, Paris, New York, Tokyo, Hong Kong and Shanghai. Good shopping conditions attract more tourists. Tourists expect comfortable environment, abundant **commodities**, dependable quality, reasonable price and good service.

Reading B

Shopping Malls

The shopping malls are designed for only one thing: encouraging people to buy. Every **aspect** of mall design is carefully **calculated** to **appeal** to the customer's psychological needs. This starts with the **overall** environment. Tests have shown that people feel most relaxed and comfortable at a temperature of 24-26 degrees. If it is any hotter, people may become

| aspect [ˈæspekt] n. 方面；情况 |
| calculate [ˈkælkjʊleɪt] vt. 计算 |
| appeal to 吸引 |
| overall [ˈəʊvərɔːl] adv. 总的来说；大体上 |
| irritable [ˈɪrɪtəbl] adj. 易怒的，性急的 |
| curved [kɜːvd] adj. 弯曲的 |
| angle [ˈæŋgl] v. 转向或弯曲成一角度 |

too lazy to walk. Any cooler, they may rush around and leave before they've spent enough money.

The choice of colors is also very important. Dark colors like orange or purple can make people feel **irritable** or unhappy. With such feelings, they are not likely to do much shopping. Therefore, very dark colors are almost never used in malls. Instead, walls are usually painted in light colors, which make customers feel relaxed and give them all a spacious feeling.

The arrangement of space in the mall is also done with great care. Research shows that most people are unwilling to walk more than 200 meters to shop. In giant malls this could be a problem. There are two ways to deal with the problem. The walkways in malls can be made **curved** or **angled** to hide their true length. Or they can be broken up by fountains, art displays or any of those other things that you thought were just there to entertain you.

Speaking

New Words & Phrases

swarm [swɔːm] *v.* 云集
sandalwood [ˈsændəlwʊd] *n.* 檀香木，檀香木色
calligraphy [kəˈlɪɡrəfɪ] *n.* 笔迹，书法
miniature [ˈmɪnətʃə] *n.* 缩小模型，缩微复制品

Dialogue A (A: visitor 1, B: visitor 2)

A: I want to look at the souvenirs over at the souvenir stand.

B: What do you need to buy?

A: I usually buy myself some jewelry or some clothing.

B: I always buy a lot of things for my family. How about you?

A: Oh yes, they practically **swarm** me when I get home!

B: What are some of their favorite gifts?

A: The teenagers like me to bring them T-shirts that you can't get anywhere else.

B: This stuff is pretty expensive, isn't it?

A: Souvenirs cost a lot for what they are, but we can shop around for better prices.

B: Let's go across the street and see what they have over there.

Dialogue B (A: shop assistant, B: visitor)

A: Is there anything I can do for you?

B: I'm trying to choose a gift.

A: Did you have anything particular in mind?

B: No, but I'd like to get something typical in this region.

A: Well, we have some handmade products. Let me show you some.

B: They're quite nice. But I'm afraid they're quite a bit expensive.

A: About how much were you planning to spend?

B: No more than one hundred *yuan*.

A: Oh, in that case, this one is OK.

B: Oh, it's perfect. I think I'll take it. Would you wrap it, please?

A: OK. Wait for a moment, please.

Dialogue C (A: shop assistant, B: visitor)

A: What can I do for you?

B: I want to buy some handicrafts as souvenirs for my family and relatives.

A: We have quite a wide variety of handicrafts here. What do you have in mind?

B: I'd like something typical Chinese, but not very expensive. What's your suggestion?

A: You don't want anything too heavy, do you?

B: Yes. I want something light and easy to carry.

A: What about some chopsticks? They will be a good present.

B: Can you show me some?

A: Of course. This way, please.

B: Oh, they are really beautiful.

Dialogue D (A: visitor, B: shop assistant)

A: I know from the advertisement that you have a large collection of Chinese fans. I'm interested in Chinese culture. Can you recommend me some that have a Chinese cultural flavor?

B: My pleasure. We have three major types: paper, silk and **sandalwood** fans. What kind would you like to see?

A: I know little about Chinese fans. Would you mind explaining a bit more specifically?

B: OK. Sandalwood is famous for its fragrance. As for paper and silk fans, we have many patterns for you to choose from. Some are painted with Chinese **calligraphy** and poems, some are with historical figures and some are with oil paintings. Do you want to have a look at each of them?

A: Yes, please. (A moment later) Oh, amazing! How beautiful they are! I like them all very much.

B: Shall I get you one from each type?

A: No, thank you. These with paintings are especially to my taste. Is this Huangshan? The scenery is fascinating. And the oil painting on this fan is really a vivid **miniature** of Huangshan's magnificence. I'll take two of them for my friends.

B: You are really thoughtful. Here you are, sir.

A: How much are they?

B: It's 35 *yuan* for each. All together 70 *yuan*.

A: Can I have a discount?

B: Sure, I will give you a 20% discount. That is 56 *yuan*.

A: Good. Here is 60 *yuan*.

B: OK. Here are the fans you want and this is the change. Welcome to our store again.

A: Sure, thank you, bye.

Functional Sentences

 特色食品

* Do you want to buy typical Chinese products and specialties?
  你想买点中国土特产吗?
* It's a traditional product of China. 这是中国的传统产品。
* Chinese tea is world-famous. 中国的茶叶世界闻名。
* We have boxes of green tea in different quantity. 我们有大小不一的盒装绿茶。
* I want to buy some jasmine tea of high quality to bring back home.
  我要买点高级的茉莉花茶带回家。
* I can recommend you some famous Chinese-style pastries.
  我可以为你推荐一些中国有名的糕点。
* It's a famous rice wine. 这是一种有名的米酒。
* Wines stored in jars are most typical of Chinese Cultural flavours.
  坛装酒最能体现中国文化风味。
* It has a history of more than 2,000 years. 它的历史有两千多年之久。
* Beijing Roast Duck is well-known and popular. It is agreeably fat.
  北京烤鸭非常有名,备受欢迎,它肥而不腻。

 纪念品

* I want to buy some souvenirs. 我想买一些纪念品。
* I want to buy something special for my friends. 我想帮朋友买一点特别的东西。
* I'd like something unique to China. 我想买中国特有的东西。
* These wood carvings are unique to China. 这些木雕是中国特有的。
* These are real typical Chinese souvenirs. 这些都是真正具有典型中国特色的纪念品。
* You made a good choice. This tea set is unusual. 您真是好眼力,这种茶具不同寻常。
* This kind of tea tastes very good. 这种茶味道非常好。
* This is the very thing I've been dreaming of. 这真是我梦寐以求的。
* It is the best quality porcelain—the famous egg-shell china.
  这种瓷器质量最好,是著名的薄胎瓷器。
* It is well received all over the world. 它在世界各地都广受欢迎。
* The flower vases are made of porcelain and covered with tiny bamboo sticks.
  花瓶是瓷器做的,上面有细竹丝。
* Suzhou silk is velvety and the color is brilliant. 苏州丝绸柔软光滑,色泽艳丽。
* Do you have any embroidery here? 你们这儿卖刺绣吗?
* This is very famous Suzhou embroidery. It is of typically Chinese design.
  这是非常有名的苏州刺绣,典型的中国式图案。
* Chinese embroidery is reputed for its high quality and design.
  中国刺绣以其质量优良和图案美丽而享有美誉。
* These Chinese brushes are used by professional artists. So I think you will find them satisfactory.
  这些是专业画家用的中国画笔,因此,我想你会满意的。
* The background of this vase is pale blue with Chinese traditional paintings of flower-and-bird. 这只花瓶的底纹是淡蓝色的中国花鸟画。
* Are they breakable? 它们容易碎吗?
* How much would that come to? 总共要多少钱?

 Exercises

一、Complete the following dialogue.

A: We need to stop so I can shop for some souvenirs at the souvenir stand.
B: _____ ?

A: I love to go clothes-shopping when I travel or buy a new piece of jewelry.

B: The kids in my family love getting souvenirs. ＿＿＿＿＿＿＿＿＿＿＿＿＿?
What do they like you to bring home?

A: My nieces love to get little jewelry boxes like those on the top shelf.

B: Things seem to cost a lot at this stand.

A: You really need to shop around with souvenirs because ＿＿＿＿＿＿＿.

B: ＿＿＿＿＿＿＿＿＿. We could walk a few more blocks away from the beach and see what the prices are like there.

二、**Complete the dialogues with the Chinese prompts.**

Dialogue 1

A：咱们停下来看一看纪念品柜台的纪念品吧。

B：你想看什么样的纪念品？

A：当我旅游的时候,我通常喜欢带回一条特殊的项链和服装。

B：我通常给我家的小孩买些东西。你也喜欢那样做吗？

A：我的家人喜欢我旅游,所以他们喜欢我带给他们的好东西。

B：他们喜欢什么东西？

A：小点的喜欢小饰品,比如那边的小贝壳动物。

B：我想这种东西有点价格过高。

A：有些纪念品柜台比其他地方要价高,所以多逛一逛值得。

B：为什么我们不到离这个旅游点远点的地方看一看呢？

A：好主意。

Dialogue 2

A：您想买什么？

B：我想买点中国糕点,能为我推荐一些吗？

A：当然。月饼怎样？它是典型的中国食品。

B：月饼？是什么？

A：月饼是圆的,看上去像圆月,所以称为月饼,而且月饼还象征着全家团聚、家庭和睦。

B：真有意思。那我就给家人买一些吧。

A：所有的月饼一般分成两类：广式的和苏式的。

B：这两种月饼有什么区别？

A：广式月饼皮软而松、味美、馅多,而苏式月饼皮松、馅味芳香。

B：每一种给我来一点。

A：好的。给您。

三、Put the following into English.

1. 你想买点中国土特产吗？
2. 中国的茶叶世界闻名。
3. 我可以为你推荐一些中国有名的糕点。
4. 它的历史有两千多年之久。
5. 北京烤鸭非常有名，备受欢迎，它肥而不腻。
6. 我想买中国特有的东西。
7. 它在世界各地都广受欢迎。
8. 苏州丝绸柔软光滑，色泽艳丽。
9. 中国刺绣以其质量优良和图案美丽而享有美誉。
10. 这是一种有名的米酒。

四、Role play.

1. You are a tour guide who is escorting the tourists to a souvenir shop in your hometown. You are supposed to help them in buying souvenirs.

2. A tourist asks his tour guide where he can buy some souvenirs to bring back to his family. He wants to buy some tea, embroidery, silk, porcelain and some handicrafts. Please make up a dialogue according to this situation.

Future Reading

Double Seventh Festival (Chinese Valentine's Day)

The Double Seventh Festival, on the 7th day of the 7th lunar month, is a traditional festival full of romance. It often goes into August in the Gregorian calendar.

This festival is in mid-summer when the weather is warm and the grass and trees reveal their luxurious greens. At night when the sky is dotted with stars, and people can see the Milky Way spanning from the north to the south. On each bank of it are bright stars, which see each other from afar. They are the Cowherd and Weaver Maid, and about them there is a beautiful love story passed down from generation to generation.

Long, long ago, there was an honest and kind-hearted fellow named Niu Lang (Cowhand). His parents died when he was a child. Later he was driven out of his home by his sister-in-law. So he lived by himself herding cattle and farming. One day, a fairy from heaven Zhi Nu (Weaver Maid) fell in love with him and came down secretly to earth and married him. The Cowhand farmed in the field and the Weaver Maid wove at home. They lived a happy life and gave birth to a boy and a girl. Unfortunately, the God of Heaven soon found out the fact and ordered the Queen Mother of the Western Heavens to bring the Weaver Maid back.

With the help of celestial cattle, the Cowhand flew to heaven with his son and daughter. At the time when he was about to catch up with his wife, the Queen Mother took off one of her gold hairpins and made a stroke. One billowy river appeared in front of the Cowhand. The Cowhand and Weaver Maid were separated on the two banks forever and could only feel their tears. Their loyalty to love touched magpies, so tens of thousands of magpies came to build a bridge for the Cowhand and Weaver Maid to meet each other. The Queen Mother was eventually moved and allowed them to meet each year on the 7th of the 7th lunar month. Hence their meeting date has been called "Qi Xi" (Double Seventh).

Unit 5　Entertainment

Unit Objectives

Master the basic words and expressions about the entertainments;
Get some cultural knowledge about Chinese festivals;
Know the advantages and disadvantages of different types of travel.

Background Knowledge

Chinese Festivals

In the long history of about 5,000 years, numerous Chinese traditional festivals were celebrated as the memory of gods or some significant days, some of which are passed down from generation to generation, while the other **faded** away for a certain reason. The traditional festivals include the nationwide ones and the regional ones, all of which are **deemed** as a treasure to the Chinese culture. The traditional festivals are of special significance, and people always practice special traditional activities in each festival. The followings are the major

fade [feɪd] vi. 渐渐消失
deem [diːm] vt. 认为
stilt [stɪlt] n. 高跷
glutinous [ˈɡluːtɪnəs] adj. 黏性的
worship [ˈwɜːʃɪp] vt. 崇拜，尊敬
mugwort [ˈmʌɡwɜːt] n. 艾蒿
satchel [ˈsætʃəl] n. 书包，小背包
constellation [ˌkɒnstəˈleɪʃn] n. 星座；荟萃
chrysanthemum [krɪˈsænθəməm] n. 菊；菊花

Chinese traditional festivals

Festival	When to celebrate	How to celebrate
Spring Festival	the first day of the first month of the Lunar Calendar	Paste Spring Couplets; Set off fireworks; Pay New Year's visits; Share dumplings with families
Lantern Festival	the 15th day of the first month of the Lunar Calendar	Perform the walk-on-**stilts**; the dragon-dance and lion-dance; Enjoy flower lights; Guess riddles on lanterns; Eat the sweet dumplings (made of **glutinous** rice flour)
Tomb Sweeping Day	Around April 4 and April 5	**Worship** their ancestors and remove the weeds growing on the ancestors' tomb
Dragon Boat Festival	the May 5th of the Lunar Calendar	Hold the dragon-boat racing; Have the rice dumplings (zongzi); Insert Chinese **mugwort** into the door head; Paste paper-cuts; Wear perfume **satchels**.
Qixi Festival (China's Valentine's Day)	The seventh day of the seventh lunar month	Young men and women date on that night; People look up at the sky to find a bright star in the **constellation** Aquila as well as the star Vega, which are identified as Niulang (cowherd) and Zhinü (Weaver Maid)
Mid-Autumn Day	August 15th of the Lunar Calendar	Have family reunion; Enjoy the mooncakes under the wax moon
Double Ninth Festival	September 9th of the Lunar Calendar	Climb the mountains to the peak to enjoy the wonderful perspective; Admire the beauty of **chrysanthemum**
New Year's Eve	Late January or early February	Have a family reunion dinner; Set off fireworks; Stay up late

Reading A

Chinese Most Famous Arts And Crafts

Chinese works of art, with its long history, **exquisite** skill and rich variety, is a **lustrous** pearl in the treasure-house of culture and art of humankind. Chinese arts and crafts are most famous and featured in eight categories: jade carving, stone carving, wood carving, **lacquer**, **ceramic**, metal

exquisite ['ekskwɪzɪt] adj. 精美的
lustrous ['lʌstrəs] adj. 光泽的
lacquer ['lækə] n. 漆,天然漆;漆器
ceramic [sɪ'ræmɪk] n. [pl.] 陶瓷器
embroidery [ɪm'brɔɪdərɪ] n. 刺绣,刺绣品

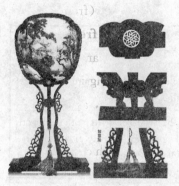

craft, **embroidery** and folk handicrafts.

Chinese ceramics have a long history. The ancient Hemudu people over 7,000 years ago were already able to make colored pottery, and people of the Eastern Han Dynasty could make ceramics over 1,900 years ago, 1,700 years earlier than the people in Western countries. With the culture advances, the use of pottery and ceramics has gradually turned from **utensils** to **ornamental** works of art.

Chinese lacquer ware boasts a history of over 5,000 years. Richly decorated lacquer made with special skill and a mixture of various **refined** colorful natural lacquer through such procedures as **polishing**, carving, filling, painting, and jade and spiral shell **embedding**, etc. **Contemporary** lacquer ware bases mainly include Beijing, Hangzhou, Yangzhou, and Sichuan, etc.

With a long history of over 7,000 years, Chinese jade carving enjoys the **reputation** of "the **essence** of **oriental** arts" in the world. The jade carving has different kinds of forms, mainly in the shape of human figures, birds, animals, flowers, and utensils. Chinese craft masters make use of the natural **texture**, shape, and **luster** of the jades and carve them into **masterpieces** of carving with excellent skills.

```
utensil [ju:'tensəl] n. 器皿,器具
ornamental [ˌɔːnə'mentl] adj. 装饰的
refined [rɪ'faɪnd] adj. 精炼[制]的
polish ['pɒlɪʃ] vt. 磨光,擦亮
embed [ɪm'bed] vt. 把……嵌(埋,插)入
contemporary [kən'temprərɪ] adj. 当代的
reputation [ˌrepjʊ'teɪʃn] n. 名气,名声,名誉
essence ['esəns] n. 精髓,精华
oriental [ˌɔːrɪ'entl] adj. 东方的,东方文化的
texture ['tekstʃə] n. 质地
luster ['lʌstə] n. 光辉
masterpiece ['mɑːstəpiːs] n. 杰作
outstanding [aʊt'stændɪŋ] adj. 突(杰)出的
sculpt [skʌlpt] v. 雕刻
adroit [ə'drɔɪt] adj. 灵巧的
grotto ['grɒtəʊ] n. 岩穴,洞室
immortal [ɪ'mɔːtl] adj. 不朽的
originate [ə'rɪdʒɪneɪt] vi. 起源于,来自
freestanding [ˌfriː'stændɪŋ] adj. 独立式的
relief [rɪ'liːf] n. 浮雕
bronze [brɒnz] n. 青铜;青铜制品
sophisticated [sə'fɪstɪkeɪtɪd] adj. 老练的;精密的
imposing [ɪm'pəʊzɪŋ] adj. 壮丽的,雄伟的
```

Chinese stone carving enjoys a long history and was famous for its **outstanding** achievements all over the world as early as in Han and Tang dynasties. The craftsmen made full use of the different colors of the stone materials and **sculpted** them into various masterpieces through **adroit** skills. The 4 major **grottos**—Mogao Grotto in Dunhuang, Yungang Grotto in Datong, Longmen Grotto in Luoyang, and Maijishan Grotto in Tianshui, whose construction began in Han dynasty and completed in Tang dynasty, are all **immortal** artistic treasure houses.

Chinese wood carving **originated** in the Spring and Autumn Period (from 770 BC to 476 BC). The techniques of wood carving can be divided into **freestanding**, engraving, **relief**, deep relief, etc. Chinese wood carving features clear cutting and smooth lines. Famous wood carvings include the Dongyang wood carving in Zhejiang, gold-lacquer wood carving in Guangdong, boxwood carving in Wenzhou, and Longyan wood carving in Fujian, etc.

Chinese metal crafts originated from the Sang dynasty (from the 17th century BC to the 11th century BC). At that time, the refining techniques of **bronze** were already very **sophisticated** and many exquisite, **imposing** masterpieces were produced and passed to later ages. Modern metal crafts mainly include **cloisonné**, ceramics, gold and silverware, jewelry, **filigree** works, as well as bronze ware and tin ware, etc.

China is famous as the "country of silk" throughout the world. It is the earliest in silkworm raising, **filature**, silk weaving and dying, and silk embroidery in the world. In the history, silk **brocades**, embroideries were exported to **Persia**, Rome, and other European countries through the famous Silk Road and played an important role in the cultural exchanges between the East and the West.

cloisonné [klwɑːˈzʊnei] n. 景泰蓝
filigree [ˈfɪlɪɡriː] n. 金银丝做的工艺品
filature [ˈfɪlətʃə] n. 缫丝，纺丝
brocade [brəˈkeɪd] n. 锦缎，织锦
Persia [ˈpɜːʃə] n. 波斯[现称伊朗]

Chinese folk handicrafts are closely related with the Chinese people's daily life. Throughout the long history, there have been developed hundreds of types and thousands of varieties of folk handicrafts. These works have greatly enriched Chinese people's life.

Reading B

Local Operas

Besides Peking Opera, known as the "national opera", China boasts more than 360 local styles of operas, of which about 50 enjoy great popularity. A

troupe [truːp] n. 歌唱团，剧团
stage [steɪdʒ] vt. 上演；举办
acclaim [əˈkleɪm] n. 称赞，欢迎

foreign visitor can enjoy at least one style of local operas wherever he travels in China. Though local operas are strongly challenged by film, TV, disco and other kinds of entertainment these days, it attracts regular audiences and companies are trying by every means to compete in the fast-changing entertainment world.

Chinese opera took shape in the 12th century. After developing for more than 800 years, it is still full of vitality. At present, the country has more than 2,000 local opera **troupes**, which **stage** thousands of pieces.

In China, a local opera form is usually popular in several provinces, while one province sees several local operas. For example, Ping Opera is popular in Beijing, Tianjin, Inner Mongolia, North China and Northeast China. In the Beijing area, not only Peking Opera but also Ping Opera, Hebei Bangzi Opera, Beijing Qu Opera and Northern Kun Opera enjoy **acclaim**.

Chinese opera is a traditional dramatic form **synthesizing** music, literature, fine arts, martial arts and acrobatics. The major difference between two local operas is changqiang (music for voices). Peking Opera and some other local operas stress singing, acting, recitation and acrobatics and their standard roles are divided into four types—sheng, dan, jing, chou—representing the male, the female, the painted face and the clown. Compared with Peking Opera, most local operas are more closely linked with the common people's everyday life and have less **stereotyped** patterns of performing. They have deep roots in the soil of real life and are well received among the people, especially the farmers.

How to **evaluate** traditional operas is a very complicated question. Some critics hold that most traditional operas are more or less linked with feudal ideas such as zhong (blind loyalty to the emperor), xiao (**filial obedience** to parents), jie (**chastity** and **virginity** for women) and yi (**code** of brotherhood to friends).

Some critics insist that we should **discard** the **dross** and select the essence of traditional operas because many are anti-feudal and reflect the ancient people's desire for equality, freedom and a happy life. But even in zhong, xiao, jie, yi, there is something in common with the traditional **virtues** of Chinese nation.

synthesize [ˈsɪnθɪsaɪz] vt. 综合
stereotyped [ˈsteriətaɪpt] adj. 固定不变的
evaluate [ɪˈvæljueɪt] vt. 评估,评价
filial [ˈfɪliəl] adj. 孝顺的
obedience [əˈbiːdjəns] n. 顺从
chastity [ˈtʃæstɪtɪ] n. 贞节,纯洁
virginity [vəˈdʒɪnɪtɪ] n. 处女性;童贞;纯洁
code [kəʊd] n. 准则
discard [dɪsˈkɑːd] vt. 丢弃,抛弃
dross [drɒs] n. 浮渣,糟粕
virtue [ˈvɜːtʃuː] n. 美德
laud [lɔːd] vt. 赞美
The Butterfly Lovers《梁山伯与祝英台》
Fifteen Strings of Coins《十五弦硬币》
redress [rɪˈdres] vt. 纠正

For example, the Yu Opera "Mu Guiying Takes Command" **lauds** patriotism; the Shaoxing Opera "**The Butterfly Lovers**" praises the pure love of young men and women; and the Kun Opera **"Fifteen Strings of Coins"** honours a sharp-sighted official who **redresses** a mishandled case.

In order to cater for contemporary theatre audiences, many dramatists have devoted their efforts to the reform of local operas and have written many excellent pieces that reflect real life. They borrow the best from other art forms to improve local operas.

New Words & Phrases

elaborate [ɪˈlæbərət, -reɪt] *adj.* 详尽的；复杂的

costume [ˈkɒstjuːm] *n.* （流行的）服饰；戏装

prop [prɒp] *n.* 道具

heritage [ˈherɪtɪdʒ] *n.* 遗产，继承物，传统

pagoda [pəˈgəʊdə] *n.* 塔，宝塔

stack [stæk] *vt.* 堆，摞

incredible [ɪnˈkredəbl] *adj.* 不可信的；不可思议的

applaud [əˈplɔːd] *vt.* 向……鼓掌

stabilize [ˈsteɪbəlaɪz] *v.* （使）稳定，（使）稳固

feat [fiːt] *n.* 技艺

mezzanine [ˈmezəniːn] *n.* 中层楼（底楼与二楼之间）

slack [slæk] *n.* 宽松的裤子，便裤

Dialogue A

Li Tao: Mike, have you ever seen a Peking Opera?

Mike: Of course. The Peking Opera is a kind of symbol of China. I suppose every foreigner would manage to see one.

Li Tao: Definitely. What do you think of Peking Opera?

Mike: Well, it is an admirable art and at the same time a difficult abstract art.

Li Tao: So it is. Peking Opera synthesizes music, drama, dancing, and acrobatics along with very **elaborate costumes** and a minimum of **props**, according to traditions and customs dating back as far as the twelfth century.

Mike: Oh, I don't know that! You guys are lucky to have such wonderful **heritage**.

Li Tao: Yes, we are. But there are not many fans of Peking Opera left. Many people are worried about its future.

Mike: That is a common problem for all classic arts. But I believe there will always be some people who like it and pass it on to the next generation.

Li Tao: So do I. Listen, let's go to see a Peking Opera together sometime!

Mike: No problem.

Dialogue B

(Mary and Bill are watching the performances.)

B: Can you see clearly? If not, we can move to the front.

M: No problem. It's very good here.

B: Look at the girl who is building a **pagoda** of bowls. She's **stacking** the bowls one by one very skillfully.

M: Oh, it's almost **incredible**. How can she do that?

B: I heard they are trained when they were very young. Oh, she's finished. Let's **applaud** her.

M: All right. What's next?

B: We have to wait for the announcer. Ah, it's bicycle **stabilizing feats** on a raised platform.

M: What's that like?

B: Er… one or more people do performances on a still bike. The bike is on a raised platform.

M: That's difficult, unless the bike is moving.

B: Yeah. It's not easy even on a moving bike. There might be a performance called trick cycling tonight. That's the one with a moving bike. If there is one, you can see it with your own eyes.

M: That kind of act would take a lot of skill. Everything is easier when you are skillful at it.

B: Yes, just like speaking Chinese. We feel it's difficult, yet the Chinese use it freely.

Dialogue C

Night Club

A: Good evening, sir. Can I help you?

B: Good evening. Could you tell me something about the night club here?

A: Sure. Our night club is on the **mezzanine** floor. It opens from 8:00 in the evening to 3:00 in the morning.

B: What's about the charge?

A: The minimum charge is the cover charge. It is RMB 80 *yuan* per person.

B: Are there any requirements for the clothes we wear?

A: Yes, sir. The club does have a dress code. Gentlemen must wear a shirt and **slacks**, and ladies are required to wear a dress or a skirt. Miniskirts are barred. Minors under 18 are not allowed in.

B: Oh, I see. Are there any exciting and interesting performances?

A: Of course. We've a live floor show featuring the six-piece rock band, the Toppers. We alternate the live show with American top 40s jocked by our professional DJ Rick Sullivan. Both the sound and the light equipment of the club are state-of-the-art. It has a nice dance floor and 2 big video screens. You can drink the best cocktails in China. The design of the club is also comparable to the best ones anywhere in the south-east Asian countries. Many guests like this cozy and comfortable furnishing. It is really, as they say, "the place to see and to be seen." Go and see. I am sure you'll enjoy it.

B: Well. It sounds attractive. Thank you for your information. I'll go there with my friends.

A: You're welcome. Enjoy yourselves.

Dialogue D

Sports

A: Wonderful. A beautiful center!

B: That's a good kick. Which side do you think will win today, China or Oman?

A: It's hard to say. The Oman team has a sharp tactical awareness, excellent team work, all-out attack and defense. But from today's performance, I do find that the Chinese team has made great progress. Now you see the Chinese No. 9 player is pushing lovely passes up the middle and out to the wings. He is trying for a goal.

B: No. 9 is Ma Mingyu. He is an excellent player. Oh, look. The ball's got into the net. The score is 1:0. The Chinese team has had a good day. I think our team will win today.

A: I hope so.

B: There goes the ref's whistle. The second half is over. The Chinese team wins. That is great!

A: I am confident that your soccer team will rapidly catch up with the first-class teams in the world.

Functional Sentences

讨论电影

* How about going to a movie? 去看电影怎么样？
* When does the movie begin? 电影什么时候开始？
* What kind of movie is it? 那部电影是属于哪一类的？
* Who is in the movie? 这部电影里都有谁啊？
* Who is the director? 谁是导演？
* Is that film famous? 那部电影很有名吗？
* The film has been shown in many countries. 这部影片在许多国家都上映过。
* I don't feel like seeing a horror film. 我不想看恐怖片。
* I can't wait to see the film. 我迫不及待地想看这部电影。
* How did you like the movie? 你觉得这部电影怎么样？
* Who do you think is the best actor? 你认为哪个演员演得最好？
* It's a well-made movie. 这是一部制作精良的电影。
* The plot is quite simple, but it has got a great theme. 情节很简单,但主题很深刻。
* That was a great movie. 那部电影太棒了。
* This movie was very touching. 这部电影非常感人。
* I cannot forget the excellent performance. 我忘不了那精彩的表演。
* In my opinion, it was the best film I've seen all year.
  我认为这是我一年中看过的最佳影片。
* The story is very exciting and full of suspense. 情节紧张,充满悬念。
* It was just meant for entertainment. 这部片子全是为了消遣而拍的。
* I guess I expected too much from the movie, so I was a bit disappointed.
  我想我对它期望太高了,所以有点失望。

欣赏音乐

* What's your favorite kind of music? 你最喜欢哪种音乐？
* I have no ear for music. 我对音乐没有鉴赏力。
* Music is not in my line. 音乐不是我的本行。
* There is a folk concert tomorrow evening. 明晚将有一场民族音乐会。
* The concert will be held in the Music Hall. 音乐会将在音乐厅里举行。

Unit 5 Entertainment

* I think it is the climax of the concert. 我想那是音乐会的高潮部分。
* This song is pretty old, but I love it. 这是一首相当老的歌,但是我很喜欢它。
* I like country music and classical music. 我喜欢乡村音乐和古典音乐。

戏剧欣赏

* Beijing Opera is popular with both Chinese and Westerners.
  京剧很受中国人和西方人的欢迎。
* There are dozens of kinds of dramas in China. 中国有几十种戏剧。
* What's on in the Opera House? 现在歌剧院里在演什么?
* There is a new play on at the theatre. It's supposed to be interesting.
  剧院在上演一部新戏,听说很有趣。
* It's a wonderful stage show. I would like to see it again.
  那是场很棒的舞台剧。我想要再看一次。
* The play has a very complicated plot. 这出戏情节非常复杂。
* In the opera, she was cast as a hard-working, up-right, middle-aged woman.
  这出戏中,她扮演一位勤劳正直的中年妇女。
* What's the most popular comedy on right now? 现在上演的喜剧最红的是哪一出?
* How is the comment about this drama? 对于这场舞台剧的评价如何?
* The next screening will begin in fifteen minutes. 下一幕将在十五分钟后开始。
* This is a beautiful theatre hall, isn't it? 这个大厅很美,不是吗?

Exercises

一、Complete the following dialogue.

A: _____?

B: Yes. Would you like to tell me what's playing for tonight?

A: Sure. There is a folk concert tonight.

B: _____?

A: Sorry. There are only some seats in the back.

B: Well, _____?

A: It begins at 7 pm.

B: OK, I see.

A: _____?

B：Just two.

A：OK. Fifty *yuan* for each.

B：_____.

二、Complete the dialogue with the Chinese prompts.

A：你愿意欣赏今晚的音乐会吗？

B：我非常愿意。

A：那太好了。

B：是谁演奏的？

A：是国家交响乐团。

B：太好了！我等不及要到剧院去了。

A：别着急，晚上八点才开始呢。我们先去订票。

B：好主意。我们走吧。

三、Put the following into English.

1. 去看电影怎么样？

2. 这部影片在许多国家都上映过。

3. 你认为哪个演员演得最好？

4. 这部电影非常感人。

5. 这个故事情节紧张，充满悬念。

6. 我想我对它期望太高了，所以有点失望。

7. 你最喜欢哪种音乐？

8. 明晚将有一场民族音乐会。

9. 这是一首相当老的歌，但是我很喜欢它。

10. 我喜欢乡村音乐和古典音乐。

11. 我对音乐没有鉴赏力。

四、Role play.

Situation 1：Mr. and Mrs. Smith are interested in Beijing Opera. So they ask the tour guide a lot of questions：the history and culture of Beijing Opera；when and where can they see such a performance?

Situation 2：A talk about acrobatics between Mr. Lin, the local guide and Mr. Black, the leader of the tourist group.

Mid-Autumn Festival

"Zhong Qiu Jie", which is also known as the Mid-Autumn Festival, is celebrated on the 15th day of the 8th month of the Lunar Calendar. It is a time for family members and loved ones to congregate and enjoy the full moon—an auspicious symbol of abundance, harmony and luck. Adults will usually indulge in fragrant mooncakes of many varieties with a good cup of piping hot Chinese tea, while the little ones run around with their brightly-lit lanterns.

"Zhong Qiu Jie" probably began as a harvest festival. The festival was later given a mythological flavor with legends of Chang'e, the beautiful lady in the moon.

According to Chinese mythology, the earth once had 10 suns circling over it. One day, all 10 suns appeared together, scorching the earth with their heat. The earth was saved when a strong archer, Hou Yi, succeeded in shooting down 9 of the suns. Yi stole the elixir of life to save the people from his tyrannical rule, but his wife, Chang'e drank it, thus starting the legend of the lady in the moon to whom young Chinese girls would pray at the Mid-Autumn Festival.

Unit 6 Handling Problems and Emergencies

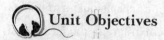 Unit Objectives

Master the basic words and expressions about handling problems and emergencies;
Get some cultural knowledge about problems and emergencies;
Know the first aid techniques of travel.

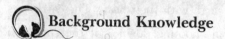 Background Knowledge

Lost or Stolen Passports

If your passport is lost or stolen, you should report the theft or loss to the local police so you can get a police report. You will need the report for insurance purposes and to obtain a replacement travel document. Some police authorities will not issue a report for lost passports. In such cases you need to demonstrate that you have at least tried to report the loss. Contact the nearest Embassy, High Commission or Consulate. Complete a Lost or Stolen Notification form in order for your passport to be cancelled. Identity theft is a growing crime. To protect your identity please bring or send this form to the police authorities as soon as possible. You do not need to wait until you apply for a new passport. It is vital you report a lost or stolen passport as soon as possible even if you don't want to replace your passport immediately. We will record the loss or theft of your passport and forward the information to the Identity and Passport Service (IPS). IPS will then cancel your passport to reduce the risk of someone else using your passport or your identity.

fraudulent ['frɔːdjələnt] adj. 欺诈的,不诚实的
tampering ['tæmpə] vi. 干预,损害 vt. 篡改
impound [ɪmˈpaʊnd] vt. 扣押
deportation [ˌdiːpɔːˈteɪʃn] n. 驱逐出境

What to do about a damaged passport

You do not need to report a damaged passport, but if your passport is damaged beyond reasonable wear and tear, some airlines may not let you travel. For this reason we recommend that you apply for a replacement as soon as possible.

You will need to send the damaged passport when you apply for a replacement. We will return it once we have established your identity and confirmed that the damage is not due to **fraudulent tampering**. 'Fraudulent tampering' means someone trying to change the identity details or photo on a passport, for example, to use it illegally.

If you later find your passport

If you find your passport after reporting it lost or stolen, you must return it to the nearest Embassy, High Commission or Consulate or the Identity and Passport Service. It will already have been electronically cancelled but we need to take further cancellation action.

You cannot use your found passport for travel. If you do your passport will be **impounded** by the Borders and Immigration Authority at ports or airports. If travelling overseas, you could face **deportation** or arrest.

You also will not be able to use it as a means of identification, as proof of nationality or for any other legal purpose as this may be detected as a potentially fraudulent act.

Reading A

First Aid Techniques

Changes in climate and time zone, long hours of sightseeing may easily cause such kind of sudden heart attack. In order to save the tourist's life at first time, you should know how to give first aid to him/her. The most common use of FATs (First Aid Techniques) is Artificial Respiration. It can be operated easily in any condition.

```
obstruct [əb'strʌkt] vt. 阻隔,妨碍,阻塞
pinch [pɪntʃ] vt. 捏,拧,掐,挤压
exhale [eks'heɪl] vt. 呼气,发出,散发
vomit ['vɒmɪt] vt. 吐出,呕吐
suffocate ['sʌfəkeɪt] vt. 使窒息,噎住,闷熄
arterial [ɑː'tɪərɪəl] adj. 动脉的,脉络状的
hypothermia [ˌhaɪpə'θɜːmɪə] n. 低体温
torso ['tɔːsəʊ] n. 躯干
cardiac ['kɑːdɪæk] n. 心脏病患者;强心剂;健胃药  adj. 心脏的;(胃的)贲门的
armpit ['ɑːmpɪt] n. 腋窝
tub [tʌb] n. 桶,浴盆
fracture ['fræktʃə] n. 破碎,骨折
splint [splɪnt] vt. 用夹板固定
```

Artificial Respiration

First, lift up the head slightly so that it falls backwards. This is to ensure that the tongue does not **obstruct** the airways.

Then, open his/her mouth and check whether the person breathes and whether there are no obstructions in the airways. Then, **pinch** the nose closed, and **exhale** air into the person's lungs; the chest will come up, check whether it goes down again. Repeat this process a couple of times. Then, put the person in the stable side position by bending the right arm so that it touches the left shoulder, roll the person over, ensure that the right arm is below the head and bend the leg. The bending of arms and legs is necessary to ensure that the person's head is positioned freely; this way if the person **vomits** he can't **suffocate.**

Bleedings

Check for bleedings. If there are any bleedings, provide pressure to the **arterial** pressure point nearest to the cut.

Temperature

Check whether the person's body temperature is correct, if, ie, a person has been in a cold environment for too long, he may have **hypothermia**. After a stressful situation, the person can also be cold due to shock. For hypothermia, we must apply heat only to the **torso**, and not to the extremeties (ie arms, legs...). This is because if too much heat was lost, the adding of heat over the entire body can cause **cardiac** arrest. Therefore we must only heat the center of the body (which houses the primary blood circuit). Provide heat by providing a hot water bottle under the **armpits**, or fill up a **tub** with hot water and have the person enter it, keeping arms and legs outside of the water. After a stressful situation (shock) we do not need to provide these measures, but only foresee a blanket.

Fractures

If the fracture is an open one and if you are skilled in this, place the bones correctly. **Splint** the broken bone(s).

 Reading B

Sustainable Tourism

Sustainable tourism is a form of tourism which involves being conscious of the potential economic, environmental, and cultural impacts of tourism. Sustainable tour companies and tourists who support the idea of sustainable tourism make extra efforts to ensure that their impact on the places they visit is positive, rather than simply neutral or negative. Several certification agencies inspect and **accredit** tour companies which offer sustainable tourism packages, with the goal of creating an industry-wide standard which makes it easier for tourists to select companies to do business with.

The concept of sustainable tourism is closely related to ecotourism, a form of tourism which focuses on environmental and ecological issues associated with tourism, but sustainable tourism is wider in scope. While sustainable tours are designed to address environmental issues related to tourism, other considerations such as the impact of tourism on the local economy are also **incorporated into** the sustainable tourism philosophy. In addition, the sustainable tourism industry is very aware of the cultural impacts of tourism, especially on local people.

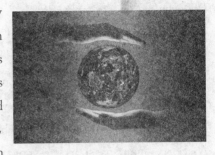

accredit [ə'kredɪt] vt. 信托，委派
incorporat [ɪn'kɔːpəreɪt] vt. (into)吸收；合并
offset ['ɒfset] n. 抵消
patron ['peɪtrən] n. 赞助人；顾客；保护人
seminar ['semɪnɑː] 研讨班；研讨会
encounter [ɪn'kaʊntə] vt. 遇见，邂逅

Companies which offer sustainable tourism typically address the concerns of their customers in a variety of ways. Many try to create tours with a minimal environmental impact, sometimes purchasing carbon **offsets** to compensate for the energy used in travel, for example. These companies also invest in the local economy, and encourage their **patrons** to do the same, promoting visits to local businesses, native craftspeople, and so forth, to ensure that more funds reach the local community.

The cultural impact of tourism is often addressed with sensitive travellers in **seminars** and classes before the trip. Such courses discuss religious beliefs, cultural traditions, and other issues which tourists may **encounter**. The goal is to allow people to **witness** and participate in traditional cultures without altering them.

Sometimes, sustainable tourism also involves an active contribution to the community. For example, tourists might volunteer with local organizations and help provide health care,

witness ['wɪtnɪs] vt. 目击，证明
donate ['dəʊneɪt] vt. 捐赠
subtle ['sʌtl] adj. 微妙的
irreversible [ˌɪrɪ'vɜːsəbl] adj. 不能倒逆的；不能翻转的

housing, and other services to needy people in the community. Others might participate in environmental cleanups or **donate** to nonprofits and charities which serve the area.

You may also hear sustainable tourism referred to as conscious or responsible tourism. This philosophy recognizes the fact that economic, social, and environmental change can be very **subtle**, gradual, and sometimes **irreversible**, placing the focus on modifying potentially harmful behaviours before it is too late.

Speaking

Dialogue A (A: staff, B: Smith)

B: Excuse me, could you help me?

A: Yes. What's the problem?

B: Well, I was wondering if anyone has turned in a passport.

A: I'm afraid not. Have you lost your passport?

B: I think so. I can't find it anywhere in my hotel room.

A: Sorry, your passport was not turned in here.

B: Then what shall I do?

A: You can fill in this lost property report, and I'll keep my eye out for it.

B: Thanks.

Dialogue B

A: I think I have lost my passport.

B: That's a serious problem. Are you sure you've lost it?

A: I'm afraid so.

B: Have you looked in every possible place that you may have left it?

A: I have searched every place that I can think about.

B: Have you taken any taxis today?

A: Yes, I've taken a taxi 2 hours ago. Oh my god, I may leave it in the taxi.

B: Don't worry. Can you remember the taxi's car number?

A: I'm afraid I can't. But I can recall its colour. It's green.

B: OK, then, we may find out which company it belongs to. And after that we may contact with the driver to get back your passport.

A: I hope so, thank you for your help.

B: It's my job. Now let's try to find out the driver.

Dialogue C

Calling the First Aid Center

(A: guide, B: hospital receiver, D: doctor)

A: Is this the First Aid Center? Please send an ambulance to 20 Tai Shan Road.

B: Is it urgent? Our ambulances are not enough to meet every call.

A: Of course. It's urgent. I think the patient is suffering from a bad wound and bleeding heavily. He may die if not treated in time.

B: All right. We'll come right away.

(after a while...)

D: Where's the patient?

A: He's there in the room. He's very ill.

D: Don't worry. We'll put him in the stretcher. You are coming with us? Step in please. Carry him into the emergency ward. Here we are.

A: I'm his guide. What's the trouble with him, doctor?

D: He had appendicitis, but is all right now that it was removed. He'll have to rest for a few weeks to recover.

A: May I send food for him?

D: No, outside food is not permitted.

A: When could I take care of him?

D: Our nurse can take good care of him.

Dialogue D

A: Get a doctor here, immediately!

B: What's the problem, sir?

A: My wife is on the floor. She's unconscious!

B: Sir, could you calm down a little bit, please?

A: Calm down?! My wife is unconscious, and you're telling me to calm down?!

B: Hold on just a second, sir. I'm dialing 911.

A: Hurry up, please.

B: I'm connecting you now, sir.

Functional Sentences

遗失护照

* I have lost my passport. Has anyone turned in one?
  我的护照丢了。有人来交过一本护照吗?
* Are you sure you've lost it? 你确定已经遗失了吗?
* Have you looked in every possible place that you may have left it?
  你是否已经在每个可能的地方都找过了?

* Have you taken any taxis today? 你今天有没有乘坐出租车？
* Can you remember the taxi's car number? 你能否记起车牌号码？
* And after that we may contact with the driver to get back your passport.
  然后我们可以和司机联系以取回你的护照。
* It's my job. 这是我的职责所在。
* Would you please fill in this lost property report? 您填一下这张遗失报告表好吗？
* I will contact you as soon as there is any information.
  一旦有消息我就会联系您的。
* I suggest you report this to police. 我建议您向警察报告。
* I think we should post a "Lost and Found" notice here.
  我想我们应该在这儿贴一张失物招领启事。
* Please describe the man that has robbed you. 请描述一下那个抢劫您的人。
* Let's look for it carefully. Maybe we can find it. 让我们好好找找，也许还能找到。

生病就医

* What's your trouble? 你怎么啦？
* Could you point out the place that you feel most painful?
  你能指出哪儿是最疼痛的部位吗？
* When did the cough begin? 什么时候开始咳嗽的？
* How is your appetite? 你的胃口怎么样？
* Do you have any vertigo, dizziness, etc? 你有眩晕、头昏眼花等症状吗？
* Has it been treated before? 以前治疗过吗？
* Do you have hypertension? 你有高血压吗？
* Was he sensitive to other things previously? 他以前对其他的东西过敏吗？
* Have you got a fever? 您发烧吗？
* When did the pain start? 什么时候开始疼的？
* Is the pain continuous or does it come and go? 疼痛是持续性的还是断断续续的？
* What did you bring up? 您吐出的是什么？
* Do you have any pain in the place where I press? 我按的地方疼吗？
* What diseases have you suffered from before? 您以前得过什么病吗？

Unit 6 Handling Problems and Emergencies

Exercises

一、**Complete the following dialogues.**

Dialogue 1

A: Excuse me, could you help me?

B: Yes. _____?

A: Well, I was wondering if anyone has turned in a passport.

B: I'm afraid not. _____?

A: I think so.

B: Oh, dear! _____?

A: This morning.

B: You'd better ask the policeman for help.

A: OK, I see. _____.

Dialogue 2

A: _____?

B: I can't stop coughing.

A: _____?

B: It started last night.

A: Do you cough up any phlegm?

B: Yes. I do.

A: _____?

B: Yellow.

A: _____?

B: Yes. I feel feverish.

A: Let me examine you.

二、**Complete the dialogues with the Chinese prompts.**

Dialogue 1

A: 对不起,我是外地人。我迷路了。

B: 你想去哪儿?

A: 您能告诉我去故宫怎么走吗?

B: 当然,沿着这条路走大约十分钟,你会看见汽车站,乘21路汽车就会到那儿。

A: 顺便问一下,门票贵不贵?

B: 不贵,门票很便宜。

A: 谢谢您告诉我。

B：没关系。

Dialogue 2

A：哎哟。

B：怎么了？你哪儿伤着了？

A：你的车撞到我的腿了。

B：严重吗？

A：是的，在流血。

B：我可以请人帮忙吧？

A：但是这儿人很少。

B：我该怎么办？

A：你可以打电话叫救护车啊！

B：对。我太紧张以至于忘了。

三、**Put the following into English.**

1. 我的护照丢了。有人来交过一本护照吗？
2. 你今天有没有乘坐出租车？
3. 您填一下这张遗失报告表好吗？
4. 我建议您向警察报告。
5. 让我们好好找找，也许还能找到。
6. 你怎么啦？
7. 以前治疗过吗？
8. 什么时候开始疼的？
9. 您以前得过什么病吗？
10. 我按的地方疼吗？

四、**Role play.**

Situation 1：At the bus station, a tourist found that his passport had lost and he needs your help. (The passport may left in a restaurant they had just have a dinner.)

Situation 2：You are an English tour guide who is calling the first aid centre for a medical care of an ill tourist.

Future Reading

Double Ninth Festival

The 9th day of the 9th lunar month is the traditional Chongyang Festival, or Double Ninth Festival. It usually falls in October in the Gregorian calendar. In an

ancient and mysterious book *Yi Jing*, or *The Book of Changes*, number "6" was thought to be of Yin character, meaning feminine or negative, while number "9" was thought to be Yang, meaning masculine or positive. So the number nine in both month and day creates the Double Ninth Festival, or
Chongyang Festival. Chong in Chinese means "double". Also, as double ninth was pronounced the same as the word to signify "forever", both are "Jiu Jiu", the Chinese ancestors considered it an auspicious day worth celebration. That's why ancient Chinese began to celebrate this festival long time ago.

The custom of ascending a height to avoid epidemics was passed down from long time ago. Therefore, the Double Ninth Festival is also called "Height Ascending Festival". The height people will reach is usually a mountain or a tower. Ancient literary figures have left many poems depicting the activity. Even today, people still swarm to famous or little known mountains on this day.

On this day, people will eat Double Ninth Gao (or Cake). In Chinese, gao (cake) has the same pronunciation with gao (height). People do so just to hope progress in everything they are engaged in. There is no fixed ways for the Double Ninth Cake, but super cakes will have as many as nine layers, looking like a tower.

The Double Ninth Festival is also a time when chrysanthemum blooms. China boasts diversified species of chrysanthemum and people have loved them since ancient times. So enjoying the flourishing chrysanthemum also becomes a key activity at this festival. Also, people will drink chrysanthemum wine. Women used to stick such a flower into their hair or hang its branches on windows or doors to avoid evilness.

In 1989, the Chinese government decided the Double Ninth Festival as Seniors' Day. Since then, all government units, organizations and streets communities will organize an autumn trip each year for those who have retired from their posts. At the waterside or on the mountains, the seniors will find themselves merged into nature. Younger generations will bring elder ones to suburban areas or send gifts to them on this day.

Unit 7　Room Reservation

Unit Objectives

Master the basic words and expressions about room reservation;
Practice the process of room reservation;
Get the information about what is reservation;
Improve writing skills to fill in the reservation form.

Background Knowledge

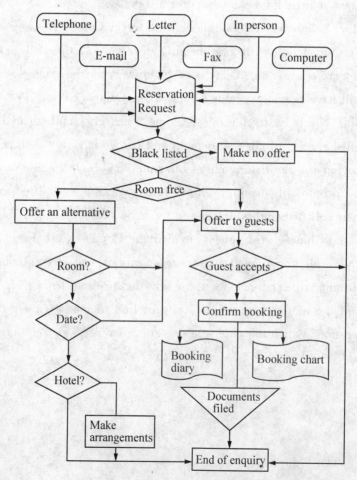

Reading A

The Hospitality Industry

The hospitality industry is part of a larger **enterprise** known as the travel and tourism industry. The travel and tourism industry is a vast group of business with one goal in common: providing necessary or desired products and services to travelers.

The hospitality industry consists of **lodging** and food and beverage operations—plus **institutional food and beverage services**, which do **cater** to the traveling public. Lodging operations **stand apart** from other travel and tourism business since they offer overnight **accommodations** to their guests. Many lodging **properties** provide food and beverage services, recreational activities, and more.

hospitality industry 酒店行业
enterprise ['entəpraɪz] n. 企业
lodging ['lɒdʒɪŋ] n. 寄宿
institutional food and beverage services 大众餐饮业服务机构
cater ['keɪtə] vt. 迎合
stand apart 自成一家
accommodation [əˌkɒməˈdeɪʃn] n. 住处
property ['prɒpəti] n. 功能
be composed of 由……组成
oriented ['ɔːrɪəntɪd] v. 以……为目的
segment ['seɡmənt] v. 分割成部分
retail store 零售商店
motel [məʊˈtel] n. 汽车旅馆
suite [swiːt] hotel 套间酒店, 指的是酒店的所有房间都是套房,除卧室还有厨房、会客室等
affiliation [əˌfɪliˈeɪʃn] n. 联系,从属关系
transient ['trænzɪənt] adj. 短暂的
residential relocation 居住空间重置
integral ['ɪntɪɡrəl] adj. 主要的

The hotel industry is part of a larger enterprise known as the travel and tourism industry. The travel and tourism industry, one of the world largest industries, **is composed of** a vast group of business **oriented** toward providing necessary and is **segmented** into five parts: lodging operation; transportation services; food and beverage operations; **retail stores**; and other related activities. The lodging operations classification consists of hotels, **motels**, inns, **suite**

hotels, conference centers, and other lodging establishments. Although the distinction among these property types is not always clear, properties can be grouped by size, target market, level of service, and ownership and **affiliation**.

Like hotels, guests can be divided into categories. Guests are typically grouped according to their reasons for travel: vacation, **transient** business, conference attendance, personal or family-related reason, weekend trips, government or military business, or **residential relocation**. The more information a hotel knows about its guests, the better it can anticipate and service their needs.

While a hotel property's architecture and style may be important in setting its theme, the front office personally plays an **integral** role in defining its image. The variety of talents and skills needed to satisfy guests' needs make front office work interesting and rewarding.

Given the increasing multicultural challenge facing hotel management, properties need to decide which markets they want to serve and establish a program to accommodate those markets. A key to guest service and satisfaction appears to be multilingual skill and an understanding of foreign customs and cultures. The enlightened manager may seek out foreign-born employees for added proficiency in serving international guests. In essence, hotels may find themselves establishing unique training programs for foreign-born employees.

Reading B

Reservation

A reservation, in the context of the front office of a hotel, means the booking or reservation of a bedroom (accommodation) by a guest and involves a particular person or persons for a certain period of time.

Firstly, with "Good morning, Welcome to our hotel, how may I help you", the reservationist should ask, "May I have your name and telephone number." If the reservation is made for somebody else, staff should ask the details of the person who is going to have an accommodation here. If the reservation is made for a company staff, the company name and company account number should be taken down.

> standard room 标准间
> junior suite 简单套房
> deluxe [dəˈlʌks] suite 豪华套房
> president suite 总统套房
> settle one's account 结账
> guarantee [ˌɡærənˈtiː] vt. 保证
> expiry date 有效期限
> official release time 官方发布的时间
> accurately [ˈækjərətlɪ] adv. 正确地,精确地

Secondly, desk clerks should take down Date of Arrival, Number of nights, and Room Type which should be clearly and carefully explained that the hotel has a variety of rooms which include **standard rooms**, **junior suites**, **deluxe suites** and **president suite**. Deluxe and Superior are divided into smoking and non-smoking. "How would you like to **settle your account**?" this is an important part about payment of the guest, which decides the reservation status of the guest. **Guaranteed**, the hotel takes the guest's credit card details (card number, **expiry date**) or full pre-payment, which means the hotel will hold the reservation for the guest until his arrival unless he cancels before the **official release time**. This is the most secure form of reservation status in theory as the hotel is guaranteed payment if the guest does not arrive. **Confirmed**, this means that the hotel has received visible evidence of the reservation. The hotel will hold the reservation until the official release time, and after this time, the hotel can sell the room to another client. In the law, visible evidence only includes a fax or letter. **Unconfirmed**, this means that the hotel has no visible evidence of the reservation.

Thirdly, ask how the guests plan to arrive at the hotel, would he like us to pick him up at the airport, or would he like us to reserve him a place in our car park which is for free. At the end, does he have any special requests? Then the receptionist should just turn over the reservation details with the guest once more. "Thank you for making a reservation with our hotel."

The staff dealing with the reservation must take the information **accurately** about the booking and record it without any mistake. She needs a professional smile on her face and to communicate politely with guests. Reservation is the first door for guests to enter a hotel, and includes a large amount of different details of different guests, if there is only a slight mistake in a reservation, the hotel could lose a VIP guest or get a complaint. Everyone must book the right person in the right room on the right night.

 Speaking

Dialogue A (R: reservationist, G: guest)

R: Good Morning. Grand Hyatt Hotel. Suki speaking, How may I help you?

G: Good Morning. I'd like to book a room.

R: May I have your name and telephone number, sir?

G: Reign Smith and the telephone number is 13940068657.

R: Mr. Smith. Is the room for yourself or the other person?

G: It's for me.

R: Mr. Smith, when would you like the room and how long would you prefer living in our hotel?

G: From May 1st to May 3rd.

R: Mr. Smith, we have standard rooms, deluxe suites and president suites. Which kind of room would you like?

G: A standard room.

R: Mr. Smith, how could you like to settle your account?

G: By credit card.

R: Mr. Smith, would you mind giving me your credit card number and the expiry date?

G: Visa 6004 2411 7965 925 to June 2015.

R: Mr. Smith, you have given me your credit card details, your reservation is now guaranteed, which means we will hold your reservation for you until your arrival unless you cancel before official release time.

G: Thank you.

R: Do you have any special requirements?

G: I would like *China Daily* in the morning.

R: Can I just quickly repeat the details of your reservation?

Mr. Smith books a standard room from May 1st to May 3rd, uses credit card for the payment and needs *China Daily* in the morning.

G: That's right.

R: Thank you for making a reservation with our hotel. We look forward to seeing you, and we hope you will have a pleasant journey. If you have any further enquiries, please do not hesitate to contact us here at the Front Office and we will do our best to be of help.

Dialogue B (R: reservationist, G: guest)

R: Good afternoon. Reservation, Jessie speaking. How may I help you?

G: Good afternoon. This is Mary from IBM Company. Could you reserve two deluxe suites for my boss?

R: For what date is the reservation?

G: From October 1st to October 7th.

R: May I know the guests' name, please?

G: That's Mr. Lee and Mr. Wang.

R: The deluxe suite room's rate is RMB 999 and plus 15% service fee for your company. Will the company settle the full account?

G: Yes. IBM Company will pay all the payment.

R: Can you confirm the details with our hotel?

G: OK, I will send a fax to you.

R: Thank you. The hotel has an official release time of 6 pm. And we will be able to hold your reservation until that time. After this, we can sell the room to another client.

G: Thank you.

R: How will they be arriving at our hotel?

G: By car.

R: Would you like me to reserve a place in our car park?

G: Yes, please.

R: IBM Company books two deluxe suite rooms for Mr. Lee and Mr. Wang from October 1st to October 7th, with the rate RMB 999 and plus 15% service fee. And the company will pay all the fees.

G: That is right.

R: Thank you for making a reservation with our hotel. If you have any further enquiries, please do not hesitate to contact us here at the Front Office and we will do our best to be of help.

Dialogue C (R: reservationist, G: guest)

R: Room reservation. May I help you?

G: Yes, my name is Steven, and I made a reservation for three nights from May 1st. I'd like to extend it for two more nights.

R: For five nights from May 1st until May 6th.

G: That is right.

R: Will there be any change in your room type?

G: No.

R: We will extend the reservation for you. And we look forward to seeing you. If you have any further enquiries, please do not hesitate to contact us.

Dialogue D (R: reservationist, G: guest)

R: Good morning. Room reservation. May I help you?

G: I'd like to reserve a room with a city view on september 5.

R: I'm afraid we are fully booked on that night. Would you like us to put you on our waiting list and inform you in case we have a cancellation?

G: No, thanks. Could you recommend another hotel near the city center to me?

R: Yes, of course. If you require a hotel as ours, I would suggest that you try the Shenyang Hotel.

G: Do you know the rate per night there?

R: I'm sorry. We don't have the exact rate but it's around six hundred *yuan* per night.

G: That sounds good. Do you have their telephone number?

R: Yes, it is 82073660.

G: Thank you very much. Goodbye.

R: Thank you for calling us and goodbye.

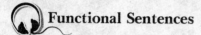 Functional Sentences

* What date would you like to arrive? 请问您的入住日期?
* How long will you be staying? 您打算住多久?
* Is it possible for you to change your reservation date? 您可不可以改变预订日期?
* Would you like standard rooms or deluxe suites? 您想要标准间还是豪华套房?
* I'd like a quiet room away from the street if possible.
  如果有可能我想要一个不临街的安静房间。
* Could you tell me the room rate, please? 请问房费多少?
* A deluxe suite with a view of sea is $1,120 per night.
  一间豪华海景套房的价格是$1,120美元。
* What services come with that? 这个价格包括哪些服务项目呢?
* The service charge is not included in the room rate. 房价内不包含服务费。
* Is there any preferential rate for the party? 团队预订是否有优惠?
* We offer 10% discount for group reservation. 团队预订可以打9折。
* How would you like to settle your account? 您打算用哪种付款方式?
* Will you be setting by credit card or cash? 您是用信用卡付款还是付现金?
* How do you plan to arrive at the hotel? 您打算选择哪种交通工具来我们酒店?
* Would you like me to reserve you a place in our car park?
  需要我为您预留停车位吗?
* Would you like me to put you on our waiting list and call you in case we have cancellation?
  我们把您加到等候名单中可以吗? 如果有人取消预订,我们会给您打电话。
* Unless the reservation is guaranteed, rooms can be sold to other guests after 6 pm. 除非是以担保预订,否则6点之后可以将客房卖给其他客人。
* We will extend the reservation for you. 我们会为您延长您的预订。
* I'd like to confirm a reservation. 我想确认一项预订。
* I'll arrive late, but please keep my reservation.
  我会晚些抵达酒店,请保留我的房间。

Task 1   Reservation Form

为了确保客人顺利入住酒店,根据国际惯例,客人须提前预订房间,一般情况下都是通过电话、网络或传真来预订。对酒店工作人员来说,要确保填写订单准确无误、快捷清楚。

填写酒店预订单应注意的事项:

(1) 涵盖个人资料。个人资料包括客人的姓名、单位、国籍、城市、地址、电话、传真、电子信箱和证件等内容,由于客人来自不同的国家和地区,同名同姓的人较多,为了避免可能出现的误解,填写预订单时,一定要做到准确无误。

(2) 清楚登记客人的要求。为了客人的方便,同时也为了酒店的有效管理,填写预订单时,务必明确客人进店和离店的时间,房间类型,是否有特殊要求等。

客房预订单 Reservation Form

☐ 新预订 New Booking   ☐ 确认 Confirmation
☐ 变更 Amendment   ☐ Cancellation 取消

Thank you for your support to the Shenyang Hotel, We are pleased to confirm your reservations as follows:

Guest Name: _____
Company: _____
Address: _____
City: _____
Country: _____
Tel: _____
Fax: _____
Email: _____
Arrival Date: _____   Arrival Flight/Time: _____
Departure Date: _____   Departure Flight/Time: _____

房间类型 Room Type	门市价 Normal Rate	特惠房价 * Special Rate (Net)	间数 No. of Room
standard room	RMB 1,188	RMB 550	
junior suite	RMB 1,288	RMB 600	
deluxe suite	RMB 1,388	RMB 650	
president suite	RMB 1,688	RMB 750	

All rates are inclusive of buffet breakfast, taxes and service charges.
Special Request:
Payment:
☐ All charges on Guest's own account 客人自付
☐ All charges on Company's own account 公司支付所有费用
☐ Room rate charge on Company's Account, incidental charges on Guest's account 房费转公司付,其他费用客人自付
** All Reservation will be held till 6pm and subject to automatic release unless guaranteed by guest's credit card, or Company (with hotel credit facilities) agrees to pay one-night room charge in the event the indicated person fails to check in on the arrival date. (☑): means confirmed item. Credit Type
Card No.
Expiry Date
　　We are looking forward to welcoming the guests to the Shenyang Hotel.

Exercise:

Fill in the Reservation Form according to the given information.

　　澳大利亚人 Tom Smith 来自澳大利亚 ABC 公司,想通过网络预订沈阳酒店。他到达的时间是 2011 年 5 月 8 日上午 9 点,到达沈阳桃仙机场。5 月 12 日下午 4 点离开。他需要一标准间。他家住悉尼市马克大街 108 号,电子邮箱是 sn@jame.com,电话:12345678,传真:12345654,护照号是 01234567。

Task 2　　　　**Hotel Confirmation Correspondence 饭店确认信函**
　　一个饭店的订房部员工不仅要能读懂相关信函,更有必要掌握各种确认函的写作技巧,如确认信、确认传真等。下面以一个发给饭店订房部的传真预订函为例,说明确认信和确认传真的写作要点。

ABC Travel Agency

New York　Fax:031-5678901

Date:May 15, 2011
To:Shenyang Hotel, Shenyang, China.
From:Mr. Tom Smith, sales manager, ABC Travel Agency, New York
Subject:Room Reservation
Message:Pls arrange one standard room for 3 nights from May 25,2011

Unit 7 Room Reservation

确认信(Letter)

(写信人地址和日期)
Shenyang Hotel
Taishan Road,
Huanggu District
Shenyang, Liaoning
China
May 16, 2011

ABC Travel Agency(单位)

82 Street(门牌号码、街道名)

New York(城市名)

USA(国家)

Dear Mr. Smith,(称谓)

RE: Room Reservation(主题)

  Thank you for your fax of May 15. We have, as requested, reserved for you: one standard room for 3 nights from May 25, 2011 to 28 at RMB 550 per night.

  If there is anything additional we can do for you and the president, please do let us know. We appreciate the opportunity to be of any help to you.(正文)

Sincerely yours,(客套语)
Shenyang Hotel(单位)
(手写签名)
Zhang Wei(打印签名)
Reservations Department(部门)

确认传真(Fax)

Shenyang Hotel
Taishan Road, Huanggu District
Shenyang, Liaoning, China Fax: 024-86688277

Fax to: Mr. Smith,(收信人)

ABC Travel Agency(单位)

82 Street(门牌号码、街道名)

New York(城市名)

USA(国家)

May 16, 2011

RE: Room Reservation(主题)

  We are pleased to confirm your reservation: one standard room for 3 nights from

May 25, to 28 at RMB 550 per night.

If there is anything additional we can do for you and the president, please do let us know. We appreciate the opportunity to be of any help to you.（正文）

Sincerely yours,（客套语）
（手写签名）
Zhang Wei（打印签名）
Reservations Department（部门）

Exercise:

You've just received a fax booking as shown in the following. Write a fax confirmation in your real room for Shenyang Hotel.

Fax to: Shenyang Hotel, Taishan Road, Huanggu District, Shenyang, Liaoning.

Fax No. 66227788

June 15

Message: Please reserve two junior suites for three nights from June 20. Please guarantee—Credit Card number 12345432167.

Thanks

Tom Smith.

 **Exercises**

一、**Complete the following dialogue.**

(R: reservationist, G: guest)

R: Good morning. Reservation, _____?

G: Good morning, I'd like to make a group reservation in your hotel.

R: May I know the name of the group?

G: The ABC Delegation.

R: May I have your names?

G: Tom is the representative of the delegation.

R: _____?

G: 20 persons.

R: We have double rooms with two beds, standard rooms with king beds, deluxe suites. _____?

G: Ten double rooms.

R: For which dates?

G: From May 1st to May 5th.

R: One moment, please, sir. The ABC Delegation needs ten double rooms with two beds from May 1st to May 5th. And we can confirm them for those days.

G: Thank you.

R: _____?

G: By plane, CZ601. Could you meet us at the airport?

R: _____.

G: Thank you.

二、**Complete the dialogue with the Chinese prompts.**

R: 早上好，预订部。很高兴为您效劳。

G: 早上好，我先预订一间房。

R: 您喜欢什么样的房间？

G: 我想要一间能看见湖泊的房间。

R: 很抱歉，我们的空房全都是面向城市的，并非湖泊。

G: 让我考虑一下，我稍后通知你。

R: 您介意留下您的联系方式吗？如果我们有面向湖泊的房间给您打电话。

G: 太好了。我的名字是张毅，电话号码13640086699。

R: 谢谢您的来电。再见。

三、**Put the following into English.**

1. 恐怕那天晚上各种类型的房间都预订满了。现在是旅游旺季。

2. 对不起，我们已经客满了，但是我可以介绍您去沈阳酒店，那里有空房。

3. 您可不可以改变预订日期？

4. 豪华套房每晚人民币1 999元，另外还要加10%的服务费。

5. 一间海景房的价格为每晚人民币2 999元。

6. 我们会尽快传真给您以确认您的预订。

7. 我想取消一项预订。

8. 我们提供免费的机场接送服务。

9. 您要什么样的房间？

10. 期待您的光临。

四、**Role play.**

Student A: You are a guest. You phone to a hotel to make a room reservation for yourself.

Student B: You are the hotel clerk. You answer the phone and make a room reservation for him.

Future Reading

Marriott Hotel

John Willard Marriott (September 17, 1900—August 13, 1985) was an American entrepreneur and businessman. He was the founder of the Marriott Corporation (which became Marriott International in 1993), the parent company of one of the world's largest hospitality, hotel chains and food services companies. His company rose from a small root beer stand in Washington D. C. in 1927 to a chain of family restaurants by 1932, to his first motel in 1957. By the time he died, the Marriott company operated 1,400 restaurants and 143 hotels and resorts worldwide, including two theme parks, earned USD $4.5 billion in revenue annually with 154,600 employees. The company's interests even extended to a line of cruise ships.

History of the Chain

In 1927, John Willard Marriott founded A&W Root Beer franchises for Washington, D. C.; Baltimore, Maryland; and Richmond, Virginia; he then moved to Washington to open a nine-stool root beer stand there with his business partner, Hugh Colton. They opened on May 20, 1927 at 3128 14th Street, NW. He returned to Utah two weeks later, and married Alice Sheets on June 9, 1927. With the approach of cooler Autumn months, and with the addition of Mexican food items to the menu, the stand became The Hot Shoppe, a popular family restaurant. In 1928, he opened the first drive-in east of the Mississippi, and the business was incorporated as Hot Shoppes, Inc. in Delaware in 1929. During the Second World War, the business expanded to include the management of food services in defense plants and government buildings, such as the U. S. Treasury.

Marriott's restaurant chain grew, and the company went public in 1953. In 1957, he expanded his business to hotels, opening the first Marriott hotel—actually a motel, the Twin Bridges Motor Lodge—in Arlington, Virginia. The company became Marriott, Inc. in 1967. Two large chains were added to the group, the Big Boy family restaurants in 1967 and Roy Rogers Family Restaurants in 1968.

Over the years, Marriott's company interests expanded. Continuing with food services, Marriott eventually invented airline in-flight food service. This segment of the enterprise continues to be a large part of their business, providing food services to many major airlines. Marriott also provides food services to many colleges, elementary schools and other venues.

Marriott was an energetic worker and rarely rested, preferring to run his company. Many attested to the fact that he ate, lived, breathed and dreamed about how to run and improve his company.

Unit 8　Reception Service

Unit Objectives

Master the basic words and expressions about Reception service;
Introduce the information about the hotel to guests in English;
Practice the process of registration;
Understand what and how to do in registration;
Improve writing skill of filling out the reservation form and writing message records.

Background Knowledge

Before Arrival

The reception staff must be well prepared with all **relevant** check-in information for everything to process smoothly.

• Reservation form. To check guest's details, if needed.

• The **arrival list** from the booking diary is usually prepared 24 hours **in advance.**

• Room availability. Receptionists are dependent upon the relevant information received from housekeeping concerning the **status** of rooms that are free to be able to **allocate** rooms to customers immediately without waiting.

> relevant ['relɪvənt] adj. 有关的
> arrival list 到达客人名单
> in advance 预先,事先
> status ['steɪtəs] n. 情形,状态
> allocate ['æləkeɪt] vt. 分配
> folio ['fəʊlɪəʊ] n. 客人的账户
> registration form 登记表

• Key and keycard. For security reasons receptionists should explain that the keycard is a kind of identification form in the hotel, and the guest can change items of his **folio**, and **registration form** which were completed by the guest upon arrival.

• VIP list and group list

- Special requests list
- Folios

Check-in Procedure

During registration the staff must take all in need from guests, which can protect guests who go away without paying or he stole something from the hotel or other guests. In this process the desk clerk should pay attention to:

1. Friendly welcome guests with a smile and communicate with them politely.

2. Ask whether they have a reservation or not.

3. Check the guest's passport, his name, passport number, the place of issue and the date of expiry.

4. Let the guest fill out the registration form and confirm the date of departure, the room type and the method of payment.

5. Take care of the signature.

6. Allocate rooms and keys, and inform the guest of the hotel facilities.

7. Ask whether he has some special requirements. Wish a pleasant stay in the hotel.

8. Work quickly and accurately.

Reading A

Arrival

The arrival stage of the guest cycle includes registration and rooming functions. After the guest arrives, he or she establishes a business relationship with the hotel through the front office. It is the front office staff's responsibility to **clarify** the nature of the guest-hotel relationship and to **monitor** the financial transactions between the hotel and the guest.

clarify [ˈklærɪfaɪ] vt. 澄清
monitor [ˈmɒnɪtə] vt. 监视
undergo [ˌʌndəˈgəʊ] vt. 经历
be convinced of 确信
amenity [əˈmiːnəti] n. 方便设施

The front desk agent should determine the guest's reservation status before beginning the registration process. Persons with reservations may have already **undergone** pre-registration activities. Persons without reservations, known as walk-ins, present an opportunity for front desk agents to sell guestrooms. To sell successfully, the front desk agent

must be very familiar with the hotel's room types, rates, and guest services and be able to describe them in a positive manner. A walk-in is not likely to register if he or she is not **convinced** of the value of renting a particular hotel room. Once a person has registered, whether she/he has a reservation or is a walk-in, she/he legally becomes a guest. Often, the hotel's property management system can be used to quickly identify available rooms and **amenities**. An electronic reservation record, created during the pre-registration application or at the time of check-in, is essential to make efficient front office operation. A registration record includes information about the guest's intended method of payment, the planned length of stay, and any special guest needs such as a **rollaway bed** or a child's **crib**. It should also include the guest's billing address, email address, and telephone number.

When the guest presents a form of identification, it serves as **proof** of intent to establish an innkeeper-guest relationship. For example, presenting a **valid** credit card during registration is deemed evidence of the traveler's intent to become a guest. The innkeeper-guest relationship has many legal benefits for both the hotel and the guest. Included in these benefits, the hotel obtains legal **assurance** of payment for the room and services provided, while the guest obtains legal assurance of personal safety while on the **premises**.

rollaway bed 折叠床
crib [krɪb] n. 有围栏的童床
proof [pruːf] n. 证据,证明
valid ['vælɪd] adj. 有效的
assurance [əˈʃʊərəns] n. 信心;保证
premise ['premɪs] n. 前提;假定
requisite ['rekwɪzɪt] adj. 需要的;必要的
enhance [ɪnˈhɑːns] vt. 提高,增加,加强
capture ['kæptʃə] vt. 俘房,捕获;夺得
deferred payment 推迟付款
debit card 借记卡
smart card 智能卡;房卡
alternative [ɔːlˈtɜːnətɪv] adj. 可用以代替其他事物的
outset ['aʊtset] n. 开始,开端
escort ['eskɔːt] vt. 护送,护卫

Gathering all **requisite** information in detail at the time of reservation and registration **enhances** the front office's ability to satisfy special guest needs, forecast room occupancies, and settle guest accounts properly.

Once a registration record is created, the front desk agent turns his or her attention to identifying the guest's method of payment. The hotel guest accounting cycle depends on **captured** information to ensure **deferred payment** for rendered services. Whether the guest uses cashes, personal checks, credit cards, **debit cards**, **smart cards**, or some **alternative** method of payment, the front office must take measures to ensure eventual payment. A proper credit check at the **outset** of a transaction greatly reduces the potential for subsequent settlement problems. If a guest has not secured management approval of credit before arriving at the property, the hotel may deny the guest's request for credit at the time of check-in.

Registration is completed once payment and the guest's departure date have been established. The guest is issued a room key and allowed to proceed to the room without assistance, or a uniformed service person may **escort** the guest to the room.

Reading B

The Black List

A back list is simply a record of people whom the hotel does not wish to accept as guests. It may be kept in book form or as a set of **loose-leaf** entries. There are only two essential requirements:

It should be easy to consult.

It should NOT be **accessible** to guests.

There are a number of ways in which individuals can find themselves on a black list:

They may have stayed at your hotel before and then 'skipped'(i. e. run off without paying their bill). You might think that such a person won't come back, or use the same if CAN happen, especially if he thinks your security system is so poor that you won't **spot** him the second time. Alternatively, he may try the same trick at another hotel. Hotels commonly exchange information about **suspect** characters,

> loose-leaf adj. 活页式的
> accessible [əkˈsesəbl] adj. 容易取得的
> spot [spɒt] vt. 认出
> suspect [ˈsʌspekt] adj. 可疑的
> compile [kəmˈpaɪl] vt. 汇编，编制
> conjunction [kənˈdʒʌŋkʃn] n. 联合
> obnoxious [əbˈnɒkʃəs] adj. 可憎的
> abusive [əˈbjuːsɪv] adj. 辱骂的
> fixture [ˈfɪkstʃə] n. [pl.] 固定装置
> fitting [ˈfɪtɪŋ] n. [pl.] 设备；家具
> trickster [ˈtrɪkstə] n. 骗子；耍诡计的人
> obligation [ˌɒblɪˈɡeɪʃn] n. 义务，责任
> solvency [ˈsɒlvənsɪ] n. 还债能力
> notoriously [nəʊˈtɔːrɪəslɪ] adv. 恶名昭彰地
> hassle [ˈhæsl] n. 激烈的辩论
> aggravation [ˌæɡrəˈveɪʃn] n. 加重，恶化
> bona fide [ˌbəʊnəˈfaɪdɪ] adj. 真实(的)

and many black lists are **compiled** in **conjunction** with other establishments.

They may have shown themselves to be **obnoxious** in some way, perhaps by becoming violently drunk, **abusive** or quarrelsome and thereby disturbing other guests, or by damaging your **fixtures** and **fittings**.

You may suspect them of having stolen something, either from you or another guest. Confidence **tricksters** and walk-in thieves find expensive hotels happy hunting grounds, and you don't want to encourage them. You may not be able to prove anything, but you do have an **obligation** to protect your other customers.

Finally, they may be employed by a firm whose **solvency** is in some doubt. Some companies are **notoriously** slow in paying their bills, and you simply decide that it isn't worth the **hassle** and **aggravation** of trying to collect. This may seem unfair on the individual, but it is actually one of the more common reasons, for blacklisting.

What can you say when you recognize that a would-be guest's name is on the black list? Usually you reply, 'I'm sorry, we're full. Coincidentally, you are also full the following night, the following year. Such callers quickly get the message. Be careful about saying 'We don't want you because of the innkeeper's duty to accept any **bona fide** traveler, and be even more cautious about giving your reasons.

A final point is that the black list need not just be a list of persons whom we wish to reject. It can also be used to 'flag' VIPs or anyone whom you think might require special treatment.

Speaking

Dialogue A (S: staff, G: guest)

S: Welcome to our hotel, madam. What can I do for you?

G: I have booked a room in the hotel. The bags are in the trunk.

S: There are altogether three pieces of luggage. Is that right?

G: Yes. Thanks.

S: You are welcome. Have you ever been to Shenyang before?

G: This is the second time and I want to see Shenyang Imperial Palace.

S: There are a lot of places worth sightseeing in Shenyang. I hope you will enjoy your stay here.

G: This way, please. The Reception is over there. The bellman will send your luggage up to your room after you have checked in.

S: Thank you very much.

G: You are welcome.

Dialogue B (R: receptionist, G: guest)

R: Good morning, sir. How may I help you?

G: Good morning, I have a reservation for a standard room.

R: May I have your name, sir?

G: Reign Smith.

Unit 8 Reception Service

R: Just a moment, please. Well, I look through my list. Yes, I have it. Mr. Smith, you have reserved a standard room for 3 nights. The rate is RMB 660 plus 15% service charge per night. Is that right?

G: Yes, that's right.

R: Mr. Smith, would you fill in the registration form, with your name, address, telephone number and nationality? Please indicate the method of payment you prefer.

G: Here you are.

R: Mr. Smith, could you sign your name here. And may I see your passport?

G: Sure, here you are.

R: Mr. Smith, your room number is 1006. This is your key card which is a kind of form of identification when you staying in the hotel and all staff should ask for it when charging items to your folio. The key card includes such information as facilities, services, price, timetable in the hotel.

G: Thank you.

R: The bellman will carry your luggage and show the room for you. I hope you are enjoying your stay with us.

G: Thank you very much.

R: My pleasure.

Dialogue C (R: receptionist, G: guest)

R: Good afternoon, Mr. Smith. How nice to see you again. How are you?

G: Fine, thank you.

R: Did you have a good journey?

G: Yes, thank you.

R: I have prepared the same room for you as you stayed last time.

G: Thank you very much.

R: My pleasure. Please sign your name here. And here is the key of room 1006. Do you have any special requirement?

G: Could you give me a wake-up call at 6:30 am tomorrow.

R: Of course. Have a nice stay in our hotel.

Dialogue D (R: receptionist, G: guest)

R: Good morning, sir. What can I do for you?

G: Good morning. I have a reservation for a deluxe suite here.

R: May I have your name, please?

G: Alan.

R: Just a moment, sir, while I look through our list. Thank you for your waiting, sir. I'm afraid we have no record of your reservation. Where was it made?

G: That's very strange. It was made about a week ago through our travel agents at home, Peace Tours.

R: I'm afraid we have no record of any reservation made by Peace Tours in your name. Do you have a confirmation letter?

G: No, we don't. We only have a copy of our itinerary.

R: May I see it, please?

G: Here you are.

R: I'm afraid this won't be enough. One moment, please. I have to check if there are rooms available. May I suggest a family suite? We have just had a cancellation.

G: That's great. How much is it?

R: Two thousand *yuan* per night.

G: That's fine. I will take it.

R: But the room is not yet ready. Perhaps you could fill in the registration form first and then rest in our lobby for a while. We will let you know when the room is ready.

G: All right, thanks.

(After the registration)

R: Thank you. Here's our welcoming brochure with all the information of our facilities. My name is Suki. If you need any help at all, do let me know. I am at your service.

G: Thank you.

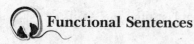

Functional Sentences

* Have you made a reservation? 您有预订吗?
* Do you have any vacant rooms in the hotel? 酒店有空余的房间吗?
* Would you fill in the form, please? 请您填写这张表。
* May I see your passport? 我可以看一下您的护照吗?
* Would you pay RMB 700 as a deposit please? 请您先交 700 元押金。
* How are you going to pay, in cash or by credit card? 您准备付现金还是刷卡?
* This is a receipt for paying in advance. Please keep it. 这是押金收据,请收好。
* Here is your key card and breakfast coupons. 这是您的房卡和早餐券。

Unit 8　Reception Service

* Here is your room card with all the information of the hotel services.

  这是您的房卡,上面有关于酒店服务项目的信息。

* You need to show it when you sign for your meals and drinks in the restaurants and the bars. 在餐厅和酒吧里用餐后签单时您须出示您的房卡。

* Please keep the key card with you at all times. 请随身携带房卡。

* You must use your room card to enter the room.

  您必须持有您的房卡才能进入房间。

* We will deliver your luggage according to the luggage label. 我们会根据行李上的标签将行李送到您的房间。

* I am afraid your room is not ready yet. Would you mind waiting a few minutes, please? 恐怕您的房间尚未准备好,请您等会好吗?

* We are very sorry for the inconvenience. 对此造成的不便我们深表歉意。

* Your breakfast coupons are in the envelopes on the desk.

  您的早餐券在桌上的信封里。

* We have a brochure of our hotel in your room.

  在您的房间里有一个我们酒店的小册子。

* Please read the emergency instructions on your room door.

  请阅读您房间门上的紧急示意图。

* If you have any valuables, you may deposit here in the safe deposit box. It is free of charge. 如果您有贵重物品,请寄存在这儿的保险箱里,这是免费的服务。

* Could you sign your name, please? 请您签名。

Writing

Task 1

Registration Form for Check-in

Surname	First Name	Sex
Chinese Name	Nationality	Date of Birth
Room No.	Room Type	Room Rate
Company	Occupation	
Type of Certificate	Certificate No.	
Type of Visa	Visa Expiry Date	
Arrival Date	Departure Date	

85

续表

Permanent Address		
Tel:	Fax:	
E-mail:		
Form of Payment	☐Cash ☐Credit Card ☐Traveler Check ☐Company ☐Others	
Please Note: 1. Checking out time is 12:00 at noon. 2. Safe deposit boxes are available free of charge at the Front Desk. The hotel is not responsible for money, jewellery or other valuables in the guest room. 3. Visitors are requested to leave guest rooms by 23:00.		
Receptionist	Guest Signature	

Task 2

Message Record 留言记录

客人到总台问讯处要求书面留言时,接待员应热情接待,填写客人留言单,注明客人姓名、房间号、留言日期,并在电脑上进行核对。经确认后,在留言单上写上留言者的姓名、单位及联系电话,并向留言者复述,经确认无误后,最后在留言单上签名。留言单一式两份,一份交由礼宾处送到客房,另一份留总台存档,以备客人查询。

```
                    Message Record
To: Mr. Green        Room Number: 1211
From: Mr. Smith
Company Name: China IBM Company
✓☐Please call back    ☐Will you meet at    ☐Will call again
A Mr. Smith said that he had come to the airport to pick you up on time, but the
plane was late. He explained that he had an important meeting this afternoon. He
asked if you could phone him as soon as you arrived here. The phone number is 024-
12345678
Taken by: Lucy    Date: June 15    Staff's signature: _____
```

 **Exercises**

一、**Complete the following dialogues.**

Dialogue 1 (R: receptionist, G: guest)

R: Good evening, sir. What can I do for you?

Unit 8　Reception Service

G: I've just arrived here. Is there any room available for this evening?

R: _____?

G: I'm afraid not.

R: Wait a moment, please. Oh, sorry. _____.

G: Where am I going to find a room at this time of the day?

R: _____?

G: Thank you. That's very kind of you.

R: I will book you into a hotel in this area. There is one room available at Shenyang Hotel. You may go there now and check in. Have a nice evening.

Dialogue 2 (R: receptionist, G: guest)

R: Good afternoon. _____?

G: We'd like to check in.

R: _____?

G: Yes. The ABC Delegation has booked 10 rooms for us.

R: We have prepared all the rooms for you.

G: Here is the name-list with the group visa.

R: Thank you. Here are the keys to the rooms. _____?

G: Yes, please. 7:00 am.

R: _____.

二、**Complete the dialogue with the Chinese prompts.**

R: 先生,晚上好。很高兴为您服务。

G: 我需要一间客房。

R: 请问您有预订吗?

G: 没有。

R: 先生,您想要哪种类型的房间?

G: 标准间。

R: 您需要无烟房吗?

G: 吸烟房需要额外费用吗?

R: 不用。

G: 如果这样,我想要吸烟房。每晚多少钱?

R: 660元每晚。

G: 如果我多住几天有优惠吗?

R: 您打算住几天?

G: 10天。

87

R：可以给您九折。

G：谢谢，我要这间房。

R：请您填写入住登记表？

G：好吧。

R：这是您的房卡。您的房间号是1012。酒店的行李员会送您到10楼。祝您晚上愉快。

三、**Put the following into English.**

1. 如果您有什么事，请打电话给客房服务部。
2. 请稍等，我查一下预订记录？
3. 请您填写这张入住登记表并交900元押金。
4. 您准备如何付款？
5. 这是收据，请收好。
6. 行李员会给您拿行李，并带您去房间。
7. 使用谁的名义预订的？
8. 很抱歉，没有您的名字做记录的预订。
9. 让我刷一下您的信用卡。
10. 希望您住得愉快。

Future Reading

Ritz-Carlton

The Ritz-Carlton is a large international hotel group with 66 hotels in 23 countries, over 18,000 guest rooms and 32,000 employees. The Ritz-Carlton name is synonymous with luxury and outstanding service. The company has very specific views and procedures relating to staff and guest relationships, being very particular to take note of guest preferences, keeping a database on guest requirements so that when guests return, staff are able to anticipate their needs. Staff at all Ritz-Carlton hotels are taught to be service professionals and to conduct themselves with dignity.

History of the Chain

The history of the Ritz-Carlton hotel company, L. L. C. originates with the Ritz-Carlton, Boston. In 1927, Edward N. Wyner, a local Boston real estate developer, was asked by Mayor Curley to build a world-class hotel. Wyner, who was constructing an apartment building and was up to the second floor at the time, agreed and changed the apartment building into a hotel. Because of the reputation of Ritz in Europe and the cosmopolitan society in Boston, Wyner knew the Ritz-Carlton name would secure immediate success. He received permission from the Ritz-Carlton Investing Company and the Ritz Paris' for use of the name and set out to create luxury in the heart of Boston. The Ritz-Carlton, Boston opened on may 19, 1927 with a room rate of $15.

The Ritz-Carlton, Boston revolutionized hospitality in America by creating luxury in hotel settings.

In the tradition of Clear Ritz, Wyner was meticulous about maintaining the privacy of his guests; a policy strictly adhered to today in all Ritz-Carlton hotels. And thus, the elite were drawn to his hotel. However, he was also very aware of the role and reputation the hotel had in the community: during the Depression Wyner kept the lights on in vacant hotel rooms to portray an aura of success.

The Ritz-Carlton, Boston was regarded as a private club for the very wealthy. Up until the 1960s, the hotel was very formal. Guests were regularly checked to see if they were in the Social Register or Who's Who and the hotel sometimes went so far as to examine the quality of writing paper on which the guests wrote to the hotel requesting reservations (if it wasn't of high enough quality, they were refused).

Dress codes were enforced for all guests, in great part due to the formality of Boston society. Restaurants were also very stringent with regard to whom they admitted. Women were not allowed to lunch alone in the café. Unescorted women were not allowed to enter the Ritz bar until 1970s.

The Cobalt Blue Goblet

Many of the Ritz-Carlton hotels and resorts worldwide continue to set their tables with the signature cobalt blue glasses. These goblets were designed to match the blue Czechoslovakian crystal chandeliers in the original Dining Room in the Ritz-Rarlton Boston. Coincidentally, blue glass was considered a status symbol in 1920s Boston. Window glass imported from Europe underwent a chemical reaction when hitting the Boston air and turned blue. Blue glass windows meant the homeowners could afford imported glass. The Ritz-Carlton, being quite fashionable, ordered glasses in this colour.

Unit 9 In-house Service

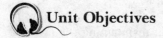

Master the basic words and expressions about in-house service;
Know how to give information about in-house service;
Get some cultural knowledge about in-house service;
Improve writing skills of Thank-you Letter and Lost and Found.

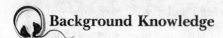

Room Status

Effective room and **rate** assignment depends on accurate and **timely** room **status** information. Typical housekeeping status descriptions include:

• Occupied: the room has a **registered** guest in it

• **Vacant**: the room currently unoccupied

• On-change: the room is currently being cleaned for the next guest

• Out-of-order: the room has a condition that does not allow it to be rented

• Slept out: the guest did not use the room but the baggage is still in the room

• Lock out: the room has been locked by the manager so that the guest cannot re-enter

• C/O: the guest has or will check out today

• OOO: out of order

• V/O: vacant and on-change

• V/C: vacant and cleaned, but not inspected yet

• V/I: vacant and inspected yet

• O/C: occupied and cleaned

> rate [reɪt] n. 房价
> timely ['taɪmlɪ] adj. 及时的
> status ['steɪtəs] n. 情形,状况
> register ['redʒɪstə] vt. 登记
> vacant ['veɪkənt] adj. 空着的;空缺的

What is Front Office?

Front office is a term used in hotels to cover the various sections which deal with reservations, room allocation, reception, billing and payments. Front office is only one of the departments within a hotel.

The first contact most would-be guests have with a hotel is with its telephone switchboard, which is part of front office. The telephonist puts the guest through to someone in the reservation department, who takes his booking and deals with any **subsequent correspondence** such as confirmations, **amendments** or cancellations.

When the guest arrives she may be assisted by a uniformed **porter**, but this is not always the case nowadays. What is certain is that he will have to go to the reception desk to register and obtain his room key.

During his stay he may well have occasion to go back to reception several times, sometimes for information or to pick up messages, and sometimes for help with tickets or further travel. He will probably have to call there at the end of his stay in order to hand in his room key and deal with his bill.

This does not end his connection with the hotel. His registration form must be kept for a specified period, and the information it contains can be used for a variety of follow-up communications designed to get him to come back at some time.

subsequent [ˈsʌbsɪkwənt] *adj.* 随后的，后来的
correspondence [ˌkɒrəˈspɒndəns] *n.* 信件
amendment [əˈmendmənt] *n.* 修正，改进
porter [ˈpɔːtə] *n.* 搬运工人；看门人

All these vitally important contacts are the job of 'front office', an American term used in place of the older word 'reception'. Strictly speaking, it only covers those staff who come into direct, face-to-face contact with the guests, the other associated sections being known as 'back office'. However, the term 'front office' is now generally used to describe the whole range of 'front of house' sections, namely:

Uniformed staff
Switchboard
Reservation

Reception

Enquiries

Bill office

Cashier

Guest relations

Occupancy

The manner in which the front office staff represents the hotel is important throughout the guest cycle, particularly during the occupancy stage. As the center of the hotel activity, the front desk is responsible for **coordinating** guest services. Among many service, the front office provides the guest with information and supplies. The front office should respond to requests in a timely and accurate way to maximize guest satisfaction. A **concierge** may also be on staff to provide special guest services.

occupancy [ˈɒkjəpənsɪ] n. 占有,使用;居住
coordinate [kəʊˈɔːdɪneɪt] vt. 调节,协调
concierge [ˌkɒnsɪˈeəʒ] n. [法] 门卫;接待员
resolve [rɪˈzɒlv] vt. 解决(答);
security [sɪˈkjʊərɪtɪ] n. 安全,保障
issue [ˈɪʃuː, ˈɪsjuː] n. 问题
interface [ˈɪntəfeɪs] v. 连接 n. 接口;交界面
revenue [ˈrevɪnjuː] n. (大宗的)收入(益);税收
posting [ˈpəʊstɪŋ] n. 过账;记账;登账
auditing [ˈɔːdɪtɪŋ] n. 审计;查账;决算
lounge [laʊndʒ] n. 休息室,娱乐室
outlet [ˈaʊtlet] n. 部门
exceed [ɪkˈsiːd] vt. 超过,越出
periodically [ˌpɪərɪˈɒdɪkəlɪ] adv. 定期地
routine [ruːˈtiːn] n. 例行公事,惯例
verification [ˌverɪfɪˈkeɪʃn] n. 证实;验证
discrepancy [dɪsˈkrepənsɪ] n. 不符合(之处),不一致(之处)

A major front office objective throughout the guest cycle is to encourage repeat visits. Sound guest relations are essential to this objective. Guest relations depend on clear, constructive communications between the front office, other hotel departments and divisions, and the guests. The hotel must be aware of a guest complaint in order to resolve it. Front desk agents should carefully attend to guest concerns and try to seek a satisfactory resolution as quickly as possible.

Security is another primary front office concern during occupancy and, to some extent, throughout all stages of the guest cycle. Security **issues** likely to apply to front office employees include guest information and the protection of funds and valuables.

A variety of transactions during the occupancy stage affect guests and hotel financial accounts. Most of these transactions will be automatically processed through property management system **interfaces** to **revenue** centers according to established **posting** and **auditing** procedures.

The room rate of the guestroom is usually the largest single charge on the guest's folio. Additional expenses can be charged to a guest's account if he or she established acceptable credit at the front desk during registration. Goods or services purchased from the hotel's restaurant, **lounge**, room service department, telephone department, transportation areas, gift shop, and other revenue **outlets** may be charged to guest accounts. Many hotels establish a maximum limit on the amount which guests can charge to their accounts without partial settlement. This amount is usually referred to as the house limit and it can be automatically monitored by the property management system. Guest accounts must be continually monitored to ensure that the house limit is not **exceeded**.

Front desk accounting records must be **periodically** reviewed for accuracy and completeness. This need is met through a system audit. A system audit can be programmed to run automatically at any time during the day. Even though computerized properties can perform the audit at any time, they almost invariably follow the nighttime tradition since transaction volumes tend to be lower during the late evening hours and most transactions occur earlier in the day.

Regardless of when the system audit takes place, room charges (room rates and room tax) are automatically posted to guest accounts as part of the audit **routine**. Other system audit tasks usually include: online **verification** of account postings, monitoring accounts against credit limits, identification of **discrepancies** in room status, and the production of operating reports.

Dialogue A (B: bellman, G: guest)

B: Good evening, sir. I am the bellman. May I take your luggage? Would you come this way to the lift, please?

(The lift door opens)

B: After you, sir.

G: Thank you.

B: Did you have a nice trip, sir?

G: It's fine. But I'm too tired. I want a good sleep.

B: I'm sure you will, sir. Our rooms are very quiet. If you need anything, just call the room services.

(After entering the room)

G: The room is facing a beautiful garden. I like it.

B: I'm glad you like it. Can I just put the luggage here?

G: Thank you.

B: There are two dining halls on the third floor and the fifth floor respectively. The former serves Chinese food, and the latter Western-styled cooking.

G: Thank you very much.

B: You are welcome. I hope you will enjoy your stay here.

Dialogue B (B: bellman, G: guest)

B: Good morning, madam. I'm the bellman. May I help you?

G: Can you show me where I can store my luggage?

B: This way, please. Is there anything valuable or breakable in the bag?

G: No.

B: Could you fill in the form and sign your name here?

G: Here you are.

B: Thank you. Here is your receipt. Show it when you claim the luggage.

G: How much is it?

B: This is free service for its guests provided by the hotel.

G: Thank you.

B: My pleasure.

Dialogue C (O: operator, G: guest)

O: Good afternoon. Operator speaking. How may I help you?

G: Good afternoon. How can I give a call to Room 1005.

O: For room-to-room calls, please dial the room number directly. It is free for our guest.

G: Thank you. How shall I get a call outside the hotel.

O: For calls inside the city, please dial 9 first and then the number. For calls outside the city, please dial 0 and then the area code and the number.

G: Thank you. And I'd like to be woken up tomorrow morning.

O: May I have your room number?

G: Room 608.

O: At what time?

G: At around 6:30 am.

O: OK, we will wake you up at 6:30 tomorrow morning. Good night, have a good sleep. If you have further inquiries, please do not hesitate to contact us.

G: Thank you.

O: You are welcome.

Dialogue D (S: staff, G: guest)

S1: Good morning. How can I help you?

G: Yes, my wallet was lost.

S1: I am sorry to hear that. I will put you through to Security Division immediately.

S2: Good morning. Security, what can I do for you?

G: Regin Smith from Room 608. My wallet is missing.

S2: Don't worry, Mr. Smith. Have you checked your personal luggage or elsewhere?

G: Yes, I've found everywhere, but I can't find it. I'm going to the airport this afternoon. What shall I do?

S2: Mr. Smith, where have you been this morning?

G: Only to the dining hall for breakfast.

S2: Let me ring the captain first. Would you please hang up and wait a moment, Mr. Smith? If any information turns up, I'll give you a call.

G: Thank you.

(after a while)

S2: May I speak to Mr. Smith?

G: Speaking.

S2: Mr. Smith, your wallet has been left in the dining hall. You may go to the Lost and Found Office now. Please remember to take your ID card with you.

G: Thank you very much.

S2: My pleasure. Have a good journey in the afternoon.

Functional Sentences

* Let me take the baggage for you. 我来帮您拿行李。

* You can get it from the Reception Desk free of charge. 您可以在前台免费领取。

* What about the daily service hour of the restaurant? 餐厅的营业时间是几点?

* Could you get me two tickets to Beijing for tomorrow here?
  你能否在这卖给我两张去北京的车票?

* Is that Mr. Smith? A lady named Mary wants to speak to you.
  请问是史密斯先生吗? 有位叫玛丽的女士找您。

* Sorry. Nobody answered. Would you like to leave a message?
  对不起,他房间没人接电话,您能留言吗?

* Excuse me, could you tell me how to get to the National Art Gallery?
  请问到国家美术馆怎么走?
* You can take No. 9 Bus and get off at the terminal.
  您可以乘9路公共汽车,到终点下车即可。
* For which date do you want the ticket? 您想预订哪一天的机票?
* Are you going by train or plane? 您是想乘火车还是飞机?
* The train to Shanghai leaves at eight in the morning.
  去上海的火车上午8点发车。
* I'd like your advice on a one-day tour here in Beijing.
  我想咨询一下北京的一日游。
* Go straight along the street to the traffic lights. You will see a tall building at the corner on your right.
  沿着街一直走到红绿灯。在右边拐角处您会看到一栋高楼。
* I hear there is a street where the local food is served. Can you tell me where it is?
  我听说这有条本地特色小吃街,请问在哪?
* Where is the nearest subway station? 最近的地铁站在什么地方?
* About a block down from here. 离这有一个街区。
* I'd like to have the paper copied. What is the cost? 我想复印,费用是多少?
* How many copies do you need? 您想复印多少张纸?
* I'd like to know if you offer interpretation service.
  请问你们这儿提供翻译服务吗?
* What language service do you need? 您需要什么语种的翻译服务?
* When do you need this service? 您什么时候需要这项服务?
* By the way, how much do you charge for it? 顺便问一下,怎么收费呢?
* There is a fax for you, Mr. Taylor. We will send it up to your room right away. 泰勒先生,有您的传真,我们马上派人给您送到房间。
* I assure to finish the document translation tomorrow afternoon.
  我保证明天下午完成文件翻译。
* The Business Center opens round the clock. 商务中心提供24小时服务。
* We offer such services as photocopy, fax, Internet, secretary, interpretation and so on. 我们的服务项目包括复印、传真、上网、文秘、翻译等。
* For outside calls, please dial 9 first and then dial the number you want.
  如果您要拨外线,请先拨9,再拨您要的号码。

Unit 9　In-house Service

* Where is the cafe, please? 请问咖啡厅怎么走?
* The travel agency in the hotel takes all kinds of booking.
  酒店的旅行社代办各种预订。
* Excuse me, could you tell me how to get to the craft market?
  您能告诉我怎么去手工艺品市场吗?
* Could you give me some suggestions on the places in Shenyang that I can go for a visit? 可以给我推荐一些沈阳的旅游景点吗?
* I will transfer your call to Room Service. Could you hold on the line, please?
  我将把您的电话转到客房服务部,请您别挂电话,好吗?
* Could you wait for a moment while I put you through, please?
  我帮您转接过去,请您稍等一会。
* I'd like to be woken up tomorrow morning. 明天早上想请您叫我起床。
* I will leave the original here. Please call me when the copy is ready.
  我把原件先放在这里,等复印好了请打电话通知我。
* Would you like me to staple these for you? 需不需要我帮您把这些装订起来?
* Shall I copy these on both sides to the paper? 我要双面复印,行吗?
* To Hongkong is 6 *yuan* per minute, including service charge.
  发传真到香港每分钟 6 元,包含服务费。

 Writing

Task 1　　　　　　　　**A Thank-you Letter**

感谢信是受到对方某种恩惠,如受到邀请、接待、慰问、收到礼品及得到帮助之后,而表达感谢之情的信函。

Dear (boss' name),

　　I appreciated the opportunity to meet with you yesterday about the position of (job title) with (company's name).

　　I really enjoyed meeting with members of the office and learning about the job. The entire team certainly seems to be highly skilled and motivated and the work itself seems as rewarding as it is challenging. I enjoyed our discussion of my opportunities and future within the firm.

　　I feel strongly that I possess the qualities required as a Room Service Supervisor. I believe my education and experiences have prepared me well for a future with you. I

97

eagerly anticipate our next meeting. Thank you for considering me for this opportunity.

Sincerely,
(Signature)

Exercise:

Translate the following into English.

亲爱的王先生:

非常感谢你们的热情款待。在这里我体会到了贵酒店的硬件设施和软件设施的实用性和合理性,服务人员的微笑服务使我感到亲切和温馨。

我相信也许下月又会再次入住酒店,祝酒店事业腾达!

史密斯先生谨上

Task 2   **Lost and Found**

在酒店范围内捡到失物而又不知道失主时,应书写失物招领启事,通告于酒店公共区域。一般来说失物招领启事写得比较简短,讲明遗失物品名称和特征,并留下联系电话。

Lost and Found

A man has just picked a wallet in the hotel restaurant and returned to the Front Desk. The owner of the wallet may go there to claim it. Please bring his or her passport.

June 6, 2010
Lost and Found

 **Exercises**

一、**Complete the following dialogue.**

(C: concierge, G: guest)

C: Good afternoon. Welcome to business center. _____?

G: I'd like to know some information on your service.

C: We can meet the needs of all our business guests. We can send faxes and do the photocopy service for customers. We have comprehensive communication facilities and secretarial assistance.

G: I would like to send a fax.

C: _____?

G: UK. What is the rate for the fax.

C: To UK, it's RMB 25.

G: That's fine. And I have some documents to be typed at the moment.

C：_____?

G：It will be about 20 pages.

C：Here is the sample of the fonts. _____?

G：This one, please.

C：_____?

G：I hope they will be ready as soon as possible.

C：I am trying to finish them.

二、**Complete the dialogue with the Chinese prompts.**

C：早上好。很高兴为您服务。

G：我想预订一天的市内游览。

C：一共几位?

G：20 人。

C：您打算什么时间出发?

G：明天早上。

C：您需要导游服务吗?

G：是的。我么需要既能用英语讲解还会德语的导游。

C：没问题,但是导游服务不是免费的。

G：多少钱?

C：200 元每位。

G：好的,我可以看看行程吗?

C：这是我们的时间表。酒店的客车明早 7 点出发,下午大概 5 点半回来。

G：谢谢。

C：我们的导游今晚会再次和您确认行程。

三、**Put the following into English.**

1. 请稍等,我去推辆行李车。

2. 我把您的行李搁在衣柜旁边好吗?

3. 谢谢您,我们不收小费。

4. 您确定在您离开前行李都打包好了吗?

5. 您要我什么时候叫醒您?

6. 您需要叫人还是叫号电话?

7. 请帮我接通 1601 号房间?

8. 如果您要拨打外线,请先拨 9,再拨您要的号码。

9. 无人接听,您需要留言吗?

10. 对不起,客人的房间电话不对外公开。

Future Reading

The Hilton Group of Hotels

The Hilton Group has had a long history, but as noted by Barron Hilton and Stephen Bollenbach, Co-Chairs of the company, in the 2006 Annual Report, the last decade had seen an almost total transformation of the company. Mid-way through the 1990s Hilton Hotels was a well respected brand name signifying large hotels primarily based in the USA and aimed primarily at business personnel seeking comfort, room size, business facilities and services while being sited at key business locations in major cities. Today the company is still oriented towards North America where 80 percent of its rooms can be found, but the size of the group has increased from 275 hotels to 2,900 around the world. Just prior to its takeover by Blackstone, the group comprised 9 brand names, namely the Hilton, Conrad Hotels, Double Tree, Embassy Suite Hotels, Hampton, Hilton Garden Inn, Hilton Grand Vacation Club (HGVC—a timeshare company), Homewood suites and the Waldorf Astoria Collection.

In total the group operates in 78 countries, employs over 105,000 staff, and seeks to operate 50 luxury hotels by 2010. Total revenue in 2006 was US $2.52 billion, which yielded a net income of US $572 million. In 2006 total capital expenditure on renovations, refurbishments and on timeshare properties equaled US $874 million. The group was founded by Conrad Hilton in 1919 with the purchase of the Mobley Hotel in Cisco, Texas. In 1930 past success with the Mobley and the Hilton (located in Dallas and built in 1925) led to the building of his first high rise hotel, then called the EL Paso Hilton Hotel in EL Paso, Texas. At that time it was the city's tallest building at 239 feet, and remains today as one of the highest in the city. An example of art deco architecture, the hotel was newly built upon the site of the Sheldon hotel that had been severely damaged by fire in 1929. It remained in the ownership of Conrad Hilton for over 30 years, in spite of the severe financial difficulties he experienced during the aftermath of the Wall Street crash and the Great Depression of the 1930s, it was not until the 1940s that the company became a national chain in the USA—indeed it was the first—a fact signified by Hilton's purchase of the Roosevelt and the Plaza hotels in New York. In 1946 the company went public with a New York Stock Exchange quotation, and three years later the company commenced its international presence with the opening of the Caribe Hilton in Puerto Rico and the formation of the Hilton international company. In the 1950s continued overseas expansion saw the company open properties in Madrid and Cairo, its purchase of the Statler Hotel Company for US $111 million and the establishment of one of the first airport hotels with the San Francisco Airport Hilton. In 2006, the relationship between Hilton Hotels Corporation and Hilton Group PLC was finally determined by the former acquiring all the lodging assets of the latter in a £5.7 billion purchase to form one of the largest hotel companies in the world.

Unit 10　Check-out Service

Unit Objectives

Master the basic words and expressions about check-out service;
Practice the procedure of check-out service;
Get the information about what is check-out service;
Improve writing skills of notes.

Background Knowledge

Procedure of check-out
- Greeting the guest
- Inquiring about the guest's stay and experience
- Inquiring about additional recent charges
- **Posting outstanding charges**
- **Verifying** account information
- Presenting the guest folio
- Verifying the method of payment
- Processing the account payment
- Checking for mails, messages, and faxes
- Securing the room key
- **Updating** the room's status

post outstanding charges 把客人在酒店每个部门的消费都记在客账上
verify ['verɪfaɪ] vt. 核实,查对
update [ˌʌp'deɪt] vt. 更新

Reading A

Departure

Guest services and guest accounting aspects of the cycle are completed during the cycle's fourth phase: departure. The final element of guest services is processing the guest out of the hotel and creating a guest history file. The final element of guest accounting is settlement of the guest's account.

At check-out, the guest **vacates** the room, receives an **accurate** statement of the settled account, returns the room keys, and leaves the hotel. Once the guest has checked out, the front office system automatically updates the room's availability status.

During check-out, the front office staff should determine whether the guest was satisfied with the stay and encourage the guest to return to the hotel (or another property in the chain). The more information the hotel has about its guests, the better it can **anticipate** and serve their needs and develop marketing strategies to increase business. In addition, it is important for the guest to leave with a positive impression of the hotel—it will definitely affect how they talk about the hotel to others and may be the determining point in whether the guest returns to the property in the future. Property management systems use registration records to automatically construct a guest history file. A guest history file is a collection of guest history records. Information in a guest history file allows the hotel to better understand its **clientele** and provides a solid base for strategic marketing. The hotel can also develop a **profile** of guest characteristics through the use of a research questionnaire.

The purpose of account settlement is to collect money due the hotel **prior to** guest departure. Depending on the guest's credit arrangements, the guest will pay cash, use a credit card, debit card, or smart card, or **apply pre-established direct billing instructions**. Account balances should be verified and errors are corrected before the guest leaves the hotel. Problems may occur in guest account settlement when charges are not posted to the guest's account until after the guest checks out. These charges are called **late charges**. Even if the charges are

vacate [veɪˈkeɪt] v. 空出
accurate [ˈækjʊrɪt] adj. 准确的
anticipate [ænˈtɪsɪpeɪt] vt. 预期(料),期望
clientele [ˌkliːənˈtel] n. 顾客,常客
profile [ˈprəʊfaɪl] n. 侧面;轮廓
prior to 在……之前
apply pre-established direct billing instructions
  申请预先制定的直接结算指令
late charge 最新消费
incur [ɪnˈkɜː] vt. 招致,遭受,引起
irritation [ˌɪrɪˈteɪʃn] n. (被)激怒
submit [səbˈmɪt] vt. 呈送,提交
outstanding [aʊtˈstændɪŋ] adj. 未偿还的;尚
  未支付的
generate [ˈdʒenəreɪt] vt. 生成,产生
isolate [ˈaɪsəleɪt] vt. 隔离
highlight [ˈhaɪlaɪt] vt. 强调,突出
evaluate [ɪˈvæljʊeɪt] vt. 评估,评价

eventually collected, the hotel usually **incurs** additional costs through billing the guest. In addition, this can be an **irritation** to the guest, who may have to **submit** an incomplete expense account to their employer. Settling accounts with **outstanding** balances for departed guests is generally transferred to a back office system to be handled by the accounting department, not the front office. However, the front office system is responsible for providing complete and accurate billing information to assist the accounting department in its collection efforts.

Once the guest has checked out, the front office can analyze data related to the guest's stay. System **generated** reports can be used to review operations, **isolated** problem areas, and it can indicate where corrective action may be needed, and **highlight** business trends. Daily system reports typically contain information about cash and charge transactions and front office operating statistics. Operational analysis can help managers establish a standard of performance which can be used to **evaluate** the effectiveness of front office operations.

Reading B

Express Check-Out

Guests may **encounter** long lines at the front desk when trying to check out between 7:00 am and 9:30 am, a **prime** check-out period for many front office. To **ease** front desk volume, some front offices **initiate** check-out activities before the guest is actually ready to leave. A common pre-departure activity involves producing and distributing guest folios to guests expected to check out. Front office staff, housekeeping staff, or even hotel security staff may quietly slip printed folios under the guestroom doors of expected check-outs before 6 am to make sure that the guest's folio can't be seen or reached from outside the room.

Normally, the front office will distribute an express check-out form with each pre-departure folio. Express check-out forms may include a note requesting guests to **notify** the front desk if departure plans change. Otherwise, the front office will assume the guest is leaving by the hotel's posted check-out time. This procedure usually reminds and encourages guests to notify the front desk of any

encounter [ɪnˈkaʊntə] vt. 遇到
prime [praɪm] adj. 首要的;最好的
ease [iːz] v. 缓和,解除
initiate [ɪˈnɪʃɪeɪt] vt. 开始
notify [ˈnəʊtɪfaɪ] vt. 通知
authorize [ˈɔːθəraɪz] vt. 授权,批准
voucher [ˈvaʊtʃə] n. 凭单,收据
crested [ˈkrestɪd] vt. 在……上加顶饰
deposit [dɪˈpɒzɪt] vt. 寄存
relay [ˈriːleɪ] vt. 传达

problems in departure before the hotel's check-out time.

By completing such a form, the guest **authorizes** the front office to transfer his or her outstanding folio balance to the credit card voucher that was crested during registration. If no credit card information was captured or no credit was established at registration, the front office generally does not provide express check-out service. Once completing the form, the guest deposits the express check-out form at the front desk when departing. After the guest has left, the front office completes the guest's check-out by transferring the outstanding guest folio balance to a previously authorized method of settlement. Any additional charges the guest makes before leaving the hotel (telephone calls, for example) will be added to his or her folio before the front desk agent brings the account to a zero balance via account transfer. Due to the possible occurrence of late charges, the amount due on the guest's copy of the express check-out folio may not equal the amount applied to the guest's credit card account. This possibility should be clearly stated on the express check-out form to minimize later confusion. When late charges are added to the account, a copy of the updated folio should be mailed to the guest so that he or she has an accurate record of the stay. In this way, the guest is not surprised when his or her credit card billing arrives with a different amount.

For an express check-out procedure to be effective, the front office must have captured accurate guest settlement information during registration. The front desk agent must be sure to relay room status information to the housekeeping department as soon as an express check-out form is received.

Speaking

Dialogue A (B: bellman, R: receptionist, G: guest)

B: Bell service. Tom speaking. How may I help you?

R: This is reception. Mr. Smith in Room 1005 is checking out. He asked a bellman to help to pick up his luggage.

B: I will send a bellman to Room 1005 right away.

(A few minutes later)

B: Good morning, Mr. Smith. I am the bellman. May I come in?

G: Come in, please. Could you take these two suitcases, please?

B: certainly, sir. Two suitcases?

G: Yes.

B: Did you have a pleasant stay with us?

G: Yes. I really like the food in Chinese restaurants.

B: Hope to see you again.

Dialogue B (C: cashier, G: guest)

C: Good morning. May I help you?

G: I'd like to pay my bill now.

C: May I get your name and room number, please?

G: Pete Black, Room 809.

C: Mr. Black you have checked in five days ago on July 9, didn't you?

G: Yes.

C: And when are you leaving?

G: Right after lunch.

C: So you will check out before 12:00?

G: Yes, exactly.

C: Just a moment, please. I will print the bill for you... Sorry to have kept you waiting. Here you are. This is your bill, RMB 2,180, including 10% service charge. Please check it.

G: That is right.

C: You have paid an advance deposit of RMB 2,500, haven't you?

G: Yes, here is the deposit receipt.

C: Thank you. This is your invoice and your change RMB 320. Count it, please.

G: That's quite all right. Thank you. Goodbye.

C: We hope you will enjoy your trip. Goodbye.

Dialogue C (C: cashier, G: guest)

C: Good morning, sir. How may I help you?

G: Good Morning. I'd like to check out.

C: May I have your name or room number, sir?

G: Reign Smith.

C: Is your room number 1006?

G: Yes.

C: Did you have a pleasant stay in our hotel, Mr. Smith?

G: Yes, thank you.

C: Have you used any hotel services or the mini-bar this morning, Mr. Smith?

G: Yes, I have taken a bottle of minimal water from the mini-bar.

Unit 10   Check-out Service

C: Mr. Smith, you checked in 3 days ago. This is the bill. The total is RMB 3,500 *yuan*, including 10% service charge. Please have a check.

G: What is this charge of RMB 50 *yuan*? Could you explain it to me?

C: That is for the taxi you called yesterday.

G: Oh, I see.

C: You have paid an advance deposit of RMB 3,000 *yuan*. And how would you like to pay other fees?

G: By American Express.

C: May I take a print of it?

G: Here you are.

C: Here is your credit card. Please sign your name on the print, Mr. Smith.

G: OK.

C: Here is your bill and receipt. We hope you enjoyed your stay in our hotel and we look forward to seeing you again.

G: Thank you very much.

C: Have a nice trip.

Dialogue D (C: cashier, G: guest)

C: Good morning, sir. What can I do for you?

G: I want to check out now.

C: May I have your name or room number?

G: Daniel Chen.

C: Mr. Chen, have you used any hotel services this morning?

G: No.

C: Here is your bill. Two nights at $99 each, and here are the meals and other services that you had at the hotel. The total is $468.

G: Can I pay it by credit card?

C: Certainly. May I have your card, please?

G: Here you are.

C: Would you sign your name here, please?

G: Is it possible to leave my luggage here until Friday. I am going to Benxi.

C: Yes, we will keep it for you. How many pieces of your luggage?

G: Just one. How much is it?

C: This is free service for its guests provided by the hotel. Would you like me to reserve a room on Friday for you?

G: Yes, please.

C: Do you want the same room type? And for how many nights?

G: Yes. For three nights. Thank you very much.

C: Mr. Chen, I have made a standard room with the city view for your on Friday.

G: That's fine. Thank you.

C: My pleasure. We hope you will enjoy your trip. See you and Goodbye.

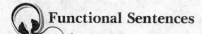

Functional Sentences

* Have you used any hotel services this morning?
  请问您今天早晨是否用过酒店内的服务设施?

* Shall I explain some items to you? 需要我解释收费款项吗?

* What is this item for? 这一项是什么费用?

* The room rate is marked at the top. 最上面那一项是房费。

* These are your international phone calls. 这些是您的国际长途电话费用。

* Here are your mini-bar expenses. 这项是您使用迷你冰箱的费用。

* Would you like a breakdown of your bill? 您要账目细分吗?

* Your bill will be paid by AA Company. 您的账单将由 AA 公司支付。

* One bill covers the room rate and telephone rate. They are paid by your company.
  一张账单包括房费和电话费,这些是由您的公司支付的。

* Would you sign your name here? 请您在这儿签名。

* This is your credit card and receipt. 这是您的信用卡和收据。

* I would like to change some foreign currency. 我想兑换一些外币。

* How much would you like to change, sir? 先生,您想换多少钱?

* According to today's exchange rate, every 100 Euros in cash comes to RMB 850.
  按照今天的汇率,100 欧元兑换 850 元人民币。

* How would you like your money? 您想要多大面值的?

* Is it possible to leave my luggage until I am ready to leave this afternoon?
  我想寄存行李,直到我下午准备走的时候,可以吗?

* May I have a receipt? 可以给我开张收据吗?

* So you have been charged for calls you did not make?
  您的意思是我们多收了您的电话费?

* I will check it with the department concerned. Would you mind waiting for a minute? 我去和相关部门核对一下。请您稍等一会,好吗?

Unit 10 Check-out Service

* I am sorry, but the bill is right. 很抱歉，账单没有错误。
* There has been an error. I neglect the detail when I draw up your bill.
  是我们搞错了，我在开账单时忽略了那个细节。
* We will correct your bill by deducting 200 *yuan* from the total.
  我们将账单改过来，从总额中减去 200 元。
* I really must apologize for the inconvenience. 我为给您带来的不便表示歉意。
* Would you like to settle the difference in cash? 您愿意用现金支付差额吗？
* Here is the money you overpaid. 这是退给您的钱。

 **Exercises**

一、**Complete the following dialogues.**

Dialogue 1 （C：cashier，G：guest）

C：Good afternoon, sir. May I help you?

G：I'd like to change some money.

C：_____?

G：Yes. Here is my key card.

C：_____?

G：Euro.

C：According to today's exchange rate, every 100 Euros in cash comes to RMB 750. _____?

G：500 Euros.

C：Well, sir. 500 Euros equals to RMB 3,750. Would you sign your name here on the exchange memo?

G：Here you are.

C：Please keep the memo, you'll have to produce it when you want to change your money back. By the way, _____?

G：Some in hundred and some in fifty, please.

C：Here you are. Please check it.

G：That's right.

Dialogue 2 （C：cashier，G：guest）

C：Good morning, sir. May I help you?

G：Good morning. I'd like to check out.

C：_____?

G：My name is Tom Smith. Here is the key.

C：Thank you, Mr. Smith. One moment, please. Here is the bill. _____?

G：That is right.

C：_____?

G：On the company account.

C：_____?

G：It's IBM Company.

C：Thank you for waiting, sir. Could you sign here, please?

G：Here you are. Thank you.

C：_____.

二、**Complete the dialogue with the Chinese prompts.**

C：早上好,先生。能为您效劳吗?

G：我是汤姆·克鲁斯。你的同事刚替我结账,但我发现账单有问题。

C：什么问题,先生?

G：我在这里从没有打过长途电话,但你们却收取了300元长途电话费用。

C：请稍等,我查询一下。

G：要等多久? 我要赶飞机。

C：别担心,先生,我们会马上查清楚……对不起,克鲁斯先生,我们的同事弄错了,这是更正后的账单及退款。十分抱歉。

G：没关系,只要弄清楚就行了。

C：谢谢您,克鲁斯先生。祝您旅途愉快。

三、**Put the following into English.**

1. 先生,今天早晨您是否用过酒店服务设施或用过小冰箱的食品?

2. 请记在我的账上。

3. 每间房每晚120美金,一共5晚,加上餐厅消费,总共是870美金。

4. 您要不要核对一下账单的数目?

5. 先生那笔是您从房间冰箱里取用饮料的费用。

6. 服务费已经包含在账单里了。

7. 公司付床费和早餐费,其他的我自己付。

8. 我们饭店每天结账的时间是中午12点,可您下午6点才退房。我们需要额外收50%的房费。

9. 请您在这里签名。

10. 这是您的零钱和收据。

Future Reading

The Accor Hotel Group

The Accor Hotel Group is one of major hotel companies operating in the world, possessing as it does 4,121 hotels with, in 2006, a turnover of £7,607 million, generating an operating profit prior to taxation and non-recurring items of £727 million. Of its total revenue 72 percent was directly attributable to its hotel operations. In 2006 the company operated in almost 100 countries, employing 170,000 people. A company based in France, that country still accounts for 34 percent of its total revenue, with a similar proportion emanating from other European countries. North America accounts for a further 15 percent of its revenue, with 10 percent coming from Latin America and the Caribbean, and the remaining 7 percent from the rest of the world. Like many hotel companies, expansion has been developed on the basis of both purchases and dispersals, as the company has sought at various times, to reinvent itself to retain both freshness in its business approach and to take advantage of new trends while establishing strong brand entities. Currently, in 2006, it sold the Compass, Carlson Wagonlit Travel and Club Mediterranee operations to better concentrate on what was perceived as it cored businesses, hospitality and services. The money generated by the sale of these strong brands helped a re-appraisal of its estate management, and led to a new policy that possesses the objective of opening 200,000 new rooms in fast expanding markets, notably in China and India. Equally the company is re-positioning itself in the market, turning its back on previous branding policies that sought to emphasize the parental name of 'Accor' to better clarify the market brands and segments of its constituent groupings with some attention being given to the Sofitel, Mercure and All Seasons brands. In total new investment of £500 million is being envisaged over the period between 2006 and 2010.

There is little doubt that China specifically features in the Group's plans for the future. The group aims to open 20,000 new rooms in a 5-year period, and thus China will account for 10 percent of the total planned new rooms being envisaged for the immediate future. The locations represent a mixture of major tourism and business centres, with 30 new properties being planned including new Ibis branded hotels in Beijing, Shanghai, Xi'an and Harbin, the last two locations being major tourism growth points, while Beijing and Shanghai appeal internationally to business, government and leisure market segments.

Pine, Zhang and Qi (2000) noted however, that many difficulties are confronting international groups opening in China, and cited a slow acceptance of foreign management methods, the impact on room rates and profits due to the fast expansion of hotel supply creating periods of over-supply and a reluctance to accept franchising or contract management arrangements given a stance by Chinese partners that ownership is more important than profits. In short, such expansion does not come without difficulties. Nonetheless Accor has made rapid progress in a short period of time. Its first property, an Ibis, opened in Tianjin in 2003, and by 2005 it had over 10,000 rooms in China based primarily on the Sofitel, Ibis and Novotel brands.

History

Accor has a history of over 40 years, and its roots can be traced to the partners Paul Dubrule and Gerard Pelisson creating SIEH and opening their first Novotel in Lille. The early success of these ventures led to a diversification strategy and in 1974 the first Ibis hotel opened in Bordeaux, while the company also diversified, for at least a time, into the restaurant business with the acquisition of Courtepaille Restaurants. In 1975 a major expansion period commenced given the size of the company at the time, and in that year Mercure was purchased, and this was followed in 1980 with the acquisition of the Sofitel chain which, at that time, comprised 43 hotels and 2 sea water spas. Further acquisitions followed including that of Tickets Restaurants—the world's leaders in meal vouchers and which, in the 1980s, distributed 165 million vouchers in 8 countries.

Unit 11　A La Carte

Unit Objectives

Master the basic words and expressions about food and beverage service in Western style;

Know how to take orders and serve a la carte;

Get some cultural knowledge about English breakfast;

Improve writing skills about the introduction of a restaurant.

Background Knowledge

English breakfast includes:

1. mineral water, ice water, orange juice, grapefruit juice, pineapple juice, tomato juice, grape juice, apple juice, **guava** juice, **papaya** juice

2. milk, **semi-milk**, **soymilk**, cocoa milk

3. **oatmeal**, **cornmeal**, corn flakes, **rice crispies**, **rye crispies**, **puff rice**, **wheaties**, **cheerios**

4. bread, toast, toast with butter, buttered toast, soft rolls, **croissant**, Danish bread, corn bread, **cinnamon** rolls, **miniature** Danish rolls, hot Danish rolls

5. butter, **assorted** jam, **marmalade**, strawberries

6. fried eggs, boiled eggs, scrambled eggs, **omelet**

7. **bacon**, ham, sausage, mushroom

8. fruit

9. coffee, tea

guava ['gwɑːvə] n. 番石榴(生长于热带)
papaya [pə'paɪə] n. 木瓜
semi-milk 半脂牛奶
soymilk ['sɔɪmɪlk] n. 豆奶
oatmeal ['əʊtmiːl] n. 燕麦片;燕麦粥
cornmeal ['kɔːnmiːl] n. 玉米片;麦片
rice crispies, rye crispies, puff rice, wheaties, cheerios 各种麦片
croissant ['krwʌsɒŋ] n. (From *French* 法) 新月形面包(用于早餐中食用)
cinnamon ['sɪnəmən] n. 肉桂
miniature ['mɪnɪtʃə] adj. 小型的,微小的
assorted [ə'sɔːtɪd] adj. 各种各样的
marmalade ['mɑːməleɪd] n. 酸果酱;(尤指)橙子酱
omelet ['ɒmlɪt] n. 煎蛋卷,鸡蛋卷
bacon ['beɪkən] n. 咸肉

Reading

Food and beverage management in hotels and quality restaurants

Hotel food and beverage management may be described as one of the most complex areas of the catering industry because of the variety of catering **outlets** that may be found in any hotel. The different types of catering services associated with hotels include the following: luxury **haute cuisine** restaurants, coffee shops and specialty restaurants, room and lounge service  cocktail bars, banqueting facilities and staff restaurants. Additionally, some hotels will provide a catering and bar service to areas of the hotel such as swimming pools, and health complexes, discos, and other leisure areas as well as often providing some vending facilities. Quality restaurants are also included as they may be discussed in conjunction with the luxury restaurants found in hotels.

Quality restaurants are those establishments whose sole business is restaurants and who offer very high standards in all aspects of their operation—an expensive a la carte menu, silver service, good quality facilities and decor, service accompaniments. The luxury restaurants found in hotels may therefore be defined as quality restaurants, although there are also those operations outside hotels which are usually independently owned and operated.

> outlet ['autlet, -lɪt] n. 【商】销路，市场
> haute cuisine [əut kwɪ'ziːn] n. (法) 高级烹饪
> license ['laɪsns] vt. 发许可证，准许

The type and variety of catering outlets in hotels will depend to a large extent on the size of the hotel. Small hotels of up to thirty to forty bedrooms may have a **licensed** bar, and a restaurant which may offer a limited hotel or la carte lunch and dinner menu. A medium-sized hotel of up to 100 bedrooms would usually have a licensed bar and two restaurants; These may include a grill room/coffee shop offering a table d'hotel menu and a separate a la carte restaurant. The bar in this size of hotels may also offer a limited selection of snacks. Today, room service in these small and medium-sized operations is limited; facilities for tea and coffee making within the room are more usually provided as an alternative. In the large hotels with several hundred bedrooms, the largest of catering outlets is found—the traditional haute cuisine restaurant alongside the more unusual specialty restaurant; lounge and cocktail bars; several coffee shops, some offering a very limited selection of snacks, other offering more substantial menu items; and varying degrees of room service.

However it should be noted that for many hotels, the importance of the food and beverage department in operating an a la carte restaurant and a twenty-four hour room service, neither of which may be significant net profit contributions, is essential for the hotel to obtain a four-or five-star grading, with their input of service and facilities enabling the hotel to significantly increase its prices for accommodation. By doing so the hotel is more likely to be able to increase its total revenue and net profit figures.

The different types of catering outlets in hotels depend not only on the size of the operation, but also on its nature and the market for which it is catering. A medium-sized resort hotel, for example, where a guest's average length of stay may be two to three weeks, may need to offer a variety of food and beverage facilities to cater for the guests' different and changing needs during their stay. A transient hotel, however, such as one situated near an airport where the guest's average length of stay may be one or two nights, may only need to provide comparatively limited catering facilities.

ally to [ˈælaɪ, əˈlaɪ] 与……结盟

The percentage of restaurants today that may be described as quality restaurants is small; indeed it may be as little as 3 to 5 per cent of the total number of restaurants in all sectors of the catering industry. However, the narrow market for which quality restaurant cater will continue to be present in the future, because there will always be that percentage of the eating-out market that demands the highest standards in all aspects of a restaurant operation, and can afford to pay the high prices charged. As for the future demands for catering services in hotels, this is closely **allied to** the demand for hotel accommodation itself. The continually growing tourism industry guarantees a future demand for some form of hotel accommodation to be provided for tourists, and with this a demand for food and beverage services.

Speaking

Dialogue A (W: waiter, G: guest)

W: Good morning, madam. Please take a seat.

G: Good morning. Thank you.

W: Did you sleep well last night?

G: Yes, I did. Thank you.

W: Would you like English breakfast?

G: Yes, please.

W: We have fresh tomato juice, orange juice, apple juice, pineapple juice and grapefruit juice. What kind of juice would you like?

G: Orange juice.

W: What would you have for bread?

G: One croissant.

W: Would you like sausage, bacon or ham?

G: Bacon, please.

W: How would you like your eggs?

G: One fried egg with sunny-side up.

W: Would you prefer tea or coffee?

G: Coffee, please.

W: You have ordered orange juice, one croissant, bacon and one fried egg with sunny side up, and coffee.

G: That's right.

W: Your breakfast will be served in a minute.

Dialogue B (W: waiter, G: guest)

W: Good evening, madam and sir. Welcome to our Restaurant. Do you have a reservation?

G: Yes, we have the reservation under the name of Mr. Smith.

W: A table for two. This way, please. How about the table near the window?

G: OK, thank you.

W: Please take your seat. Would you like an aperitif before your dinner?

G: One red Martini for my wife and one Cinzano for me.

W: Here is the menu for today. If you are ready to order, please just let me know.

(A few minutes later)

W: May I take the order now?

G: Yes, please.

W: What would you like for your appetizer?

G: What's the specialty of the restaurant?

W: How about House Salad, an assortment of avocado, lettuce & crabmeat with special house dressing?

G: My wife would like the soup and I will try House Salad.

W: Would you refer some sirloin steak for your main course?

G: OK, two of that.

W: Would you like your steak well done, medium, or rare?

G: Please give my wife medium and rare to me.

W: What would you like to go with your main course?

G: Baked potatoes and cheese cauliflower.

W: Would you like some drink with your dinner?

G: One bottle of red wine.

W: Anything for dessert?

G: One chocolate ice-cream for my wife, and one apple pie for me.

W: Your order will be ready soon. Enjoy your meal.

Dialogue C (W: waiter, G: guest)

W: Excuse me, Mrs. Smith. This is the soup for you, and House Salad for Mr. Smith.

G1: Thank you. House Salad looks good.

G2: The soup tastes good.

W: I am so glad you like them. The sirloin steak in medium with baked potatoes and cheese cauliflower is for Mrs. Smith.

G2: Thank you.

W: The sirloin steak in rare with baked potatoes and cheese cauliflower is for Mr. Smith. Enjoy your meal.

G1: Thank you. Would you give us two glasses of water?

W: Of course. Water, please.

(When the guest finishes the meal)

G1: Bill, please.

W: How would you like to pay your bill?

G1: Sign it to my room.

W: A minute, please.

(A minute later)

W: Here is your bill. May I have a look at your room card, please?

G1: Here it is.

W: Thank you. I hope you have enjoyed your dinner.

Dialogue D（W：waiter，G：guest）

W：Anything to drink，sir?

G：I'd like to have an cocktail to star with. Do you have any recommendations?

W：What about House Cocktail? It's special.

G：How do you make it?

W：It is a concoction of Remy Martin and ginger ale.

G：Please bring me the House Cocktail and one sprite with lemon for the lady.

W：Your sprite with lemon, madam. And your House Cocktail. How do you like it, sir?

G：The color is beautiful and the taste is very good. It's fragrant and refreshing. Thank you.

W：You are welcome. Please enjoy.

 Functional Sentences

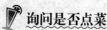 询问是否点菜

* Are you ready to order now, sir? 先生，准备好点菜了吗？
* May I take your order now, madam? 女士，现在可以点菜了吗？
* Would you like to order now? 现在可以点菜了吗？
* Have you chosen what to eat and drink? 您选好了吗？
* Have you decided yet? 您决定了吗？

 询问喜好

您要 A 还是 B?

* Which would you like, A or B?
* What would you prefer, A or B?
* Would you like A or B?
* Would you prefer A or B?

 征求意见

请问您需要什么开胃酒/头盘/主菜/牛排/蔬菜/甜点/酒水

Unit 11 A La Carte

* Your aperitif, please?
* Would you like an aperitif before your dinner?
* Would you like a drink before your dinner?
* What kind of drink would you like before your dinner?
* What would you like for your starter?
* What would you have for your appetizer?
* What would you like to begin with?
* What kind of main course would you like?
* Would you like some steak for your main course?
* Would you prefer some sirloin steak for your main course?
* How would you like your steak?
* How would you like your steak cooked?
* How would you like your steak rare, medium or well done?
* What vegetable would you like?
* What would you like to go with your main course?
* What kind of vegetable would you like with your steak?
* What will your vegetable be?
* What dessert would you like?
* What would you like for your dessert?
* What shall I bring for your dessert?
* Would you like some ice cream?
* Anything for dessert?
* What kind of drink would you like with your dinner?
* Would you like some wine?
* What kind of beer would you prefer?

菜肴推荐

* May I recommend something to you?
* Shall I recommend some local delicacies?
* Why not try the steak?

Exercises

一、**Complete the following dialogues.**

Dialogue 1 (W: waiter, G: guest)

W: Good evening, girls and boys. _____?

G1: I'd like some Irish whiskey.

W: _____?

G1: On the rocks.

G2: Gin and Tonic for me.

G3: I'd like some brandy.

W: What brand would you prefer?

G3: Cognac.

W: With soda water?

G3: Yes, please.

W: _____?

G4: I have no idea. What will you recommend for me?

W: Vodka with lemon juice for you?

G4: OK, thank you.

W: Any other drinks, please?

G2: Could you offer me one whiskey? Any brand, but straight up.

G4: I prefer some soft drink. Please give me one coke.

W: _____?

G1: Chips and peanuts, please

W: _____.

Dialogue 2 (W: waiter, G: guest)

W: Good morning, Mr. Green. _____?

G: Good morning. Could you cater for a buffet lunch we're planning to hold on Friday, the 3rd of May?

W: I think we could arrange that for you. _____?

G: There will be about 120 people. We have established good relations with the local companies. You might offer a good opportunity for us to meet and celebrate.

W: How many guests could you guarantee?

G: At least 100.

W: _____?

G: About RMB 300 with wine included.

W: I will show you three different menus with recommended wine list.

G: I want to work out a menu of our own.

W: _____?

G: Some of our friends are from America, but most of them are Chinese. So I think it would be welcome to prepare some Western food as well as some local traditional Chinese dishes.

W: We have a large variety of food and drinks for you to choose from, both Chinese style and Western.

G: OK, that's fine.

W: _____?

G: We need large tables. And we would prefer a buffet with tables and seats.

W: That can easily be arranged. Any special events, please?

G: With fine table decorations and background music.

W: That's fine. Thank you. We look forward to seeing you. If you have any further inquiries please do not hesitate to contact us.

二、**Complete the dialogue with the Chinese prompts.**

W: 下午好,欢迎光临麦当劳餐厅,请问您点哪种汉堡?

G: 我不想吃这个。你们这还有别的套餐吗?

W: 有,我们这有汉堡套餐、鸡块套餐、鸡翅套餐,您要哪个套餐呢?

G: 汉堡都有什么的?

W: 我们这有鸡肉的、牛肉的,还有鱼肉的。您想吃哪个?

G: 鸡肉的吧。

W: 辣的还是不辣的?

G: 不辣的。

W: 那我建议您吃板烧鸡腿堡套餐吧。这个是不辣的。才23元。

G: 套餐里都有什么?

W: 汉堡、薯条、可乐。

G: 行,就来这个吧。

W: 我们这有新出的蜜汁鸡翅,您来一对吗?

G: 不要了。

W: 一共是23元。

(顾客给30元)

W: 找您7元,您收好。您请到左边等餐,有专人为您备餐,吸管这边自取一下。

三、Put the following into English.

1. 您想叫一份全餐还是按菜单点菜？
2. 一般正餐包括开胃餐、主菜和甜点。
3. 我现在可以上汤了吗？
4. 先生，您的牛排要配什么？
5. 您要什么色拉酱？
6. 咖啡是和正餐一起上还是和甜食一起上？
7. 我们这儿有嘉士伯、喜力、生力、麒麟、富士达、健力士以及百威等啤酒。
8. 要不要来点小吃下酒呢？
9. 白兰地加冰还是直饮？
10. 我们这儿供应黄瓜汁、橙汁、胡萝卜汁以及番茄汁。它们都是现榨的。

Future Reading

Taj Hotels Group

For more than 100 years, the Taj Hotels Group (THG) has been providing the Indian hospitality experience to its local and international guests through the Indian Hotels Company Limited (IHCL) and its subsidiaries collectively known as Taj Hotels Resorts and Palaces. It is recognized as one of Asia's largest and finest hotel company. Incorporated by the founder of the Tata Group, Jamsetji N Tata, the company opened its first property, the Taj Mahal Palace hotel, Bombay, in 1903. the Taj became a symbol of Indian hospitality and completed its centenary year in 2003. Taj Hotels Resorts and Palaces, a part of the Tata Group of companies, comprises 59 hotels at 40 locations across India with an additional 17 international hotels in the Maldives, Mauritius, Malaysia, United Kingdom, United States of America, Bhutan, Sri Lanka, Africa, the Middle East and Australia.

The company has had a long-standing commitment to the continued development of the Indian tourism and hospitality industry. From the 1970s through the 1990s, the Taj played an important role in launching several of India's key tourist destinations. Working in tandem with the Indian government, the Taj developed resorts and retreats while the government developed roads and railways to India's hidden treasures.

Unit 11 A La Carte

In India, Taj is recognized as the premier hospitality provider, spanning the length and breadth of the country, and gracing important industrial towns and cities, beautiful beaches, historical and pilgrim centres, and wildlife destinations.

As an innovator in dining, Taj was the first to introduce China's Sichuan, Thai, Italian, Mexican, and Californian cuisine into the country. In 1972, it was the first to open a 24-hour coffee shop in India at Taj Mahal Palace & Tower, Mumbai. Today, each restaurant is reflective of that tradition, setting benchmarks for an outstanding culinary experience.

Billed by the Times, London as the finest hotel in the East, the Taj's first hotel, the Taj Mahal Palace & Tower, Mumbai was perhaps the only place in the world where a British Viceroy could rub shoulders with an Indian Maharajah, where the Congress could debate with right wing leaders, and where sailors on shore-leave could flirt with the Pompadour Follies. Built at the cost of a quarter of a million pounds, the hotel introduced a series of firsts that set new benchmarks in Indian hospitality. Over the years, the Taj brought into Bombay 'Professors of Dance' Mademoiselle Singy to raise temperatures and a few eyebrows with the Tango, the first air-conditioned ballroom to cool things down, the first cold storage, the first licensed bar, and more.

The changing decades ushered in new tastes and newer guests such as Mick Jagger, seven Spielberg, and David Rockefeller. From Nobel laureates to rock stars, fashion divas, to oil-rich sheiks, Taj represented a global village long before the term was to become a cliche. Even today, a hundred years on, guests find Taj taking luxury to greater heights in all its hotels around the world including business capitals, fairy-tale palaces, on secluded islands, in private yachts, aboard executive jets, and amidst spas and resorts.

Important Milestones in the history of Taj show that in 1971—1972 the Group pioneered the concept of authentic Palace Hotels in the country with the Rambagh palace in Jaipur, the Palace of the Maharajah of the erstwhile state of Jaipur. In 1974 Taj conceptualized the unique beach resort at Fort Aguada, Goa built within the walls of a Portuguese fort overlooking the Arabian Sea and in 1978—1982 Taj launched in Delhi its luxury hotel—Taj Mahal Motel and Taj Palace preparing India for the Asian Games with the largest convention centre in the country. In 1982 Taj established a presence in the Western Hemisphere with the historic St. James Court Hotel near Buckingham Palace, London. The group expanded in domestic and regional market from 1984 to 1992 by opening properties in Kerala and Sri Lanka.

　　The Taj group further ventured in opening business hotels in key cities and towns across the country from 1992 to 1997 and branded them as Taj Residency hotels. In 2000 the group consolidated its position as the largest chain in India with hotels in Ahmadabad and Hyderabad, the latter city being a joint venture with GVK hotels resulting in a dominant position in the market for premium and luxury hotel rooms.

　　Another milestone to note was that in year 2002 the new Taj Exotica Resort & Spa, Maldives opened and within six months of its launch, was awarded the title of 'the Best Resort in the World' in the first ever Harpers and Queen Travel Awards.

Unit 12 In Chinese Restaurant

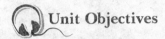

Master the basic words and expressions about food and beverage service in Chinese Restaurant;

Know how to give information about food and beverage;

Get some cultural knowledge about food and beverage information;

Improve writing skills about complaint letter.

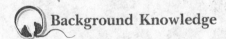

Chinese Cuisine

Shandong cuisine(鲁菜)

Braised Sea Cucumber with Scallion(葱烧海参)

Yellow River Carp in Sweet and Sour Sauce(糖醋黄河鲤鱼)

Braised Intestines in Brown Sauce(九转大肠)

Sichuan cuisine(四川菜)

Kung Pao Chicken(宫保鸡丁)

The Spicy and Hot Bean Curd/Mapo Bean Curd(麻婆豆腐)

Shredded Pork with Garlic Sauce(鱼香肉丝)

Pork in a Spicy Soup Base with Some Greens(水煮肉片)

Jiangsu cuisine(江苏菜)

Steamed Minced Pork Ball(清炖狮子头)

Jiaohuazi (Beggar's) Chicken(叫花鸡)

Sweet and Sour Fried Mandarin Fish in Squirrel Shape(松鼠鳜鱼)

Cantonese cuisine(广东菜)

Crisp Skin Roasted Suckling Pig(脆皮乳猪)

Hakka Style Braised Chicken in Gravy(东江盐焗鸡)

Deep-fried Stuffed Bean Curd(脆皮豆腐)

Zhejiang cuisine(浙江菜)

West Lake Fish in Vinegar Gravy(西湖醋鱼)

Dongpo Pork(东坡肉)

Shrimp with Longjing Tea(龙井虾仁)

Fujian cuisine(福建菜)

'Buddha Jumping over the Wall'—Sea Food and Poultry in Casserole(佛跳墙)

Litchi Flesh(荔枝肉)

Bird's Nest and Sliced Chicken Soup(鸡丝燕窝)

Hunan cuisine(湖南菜)

Spicy Chicken(麻辣仔鸡)

Steamed Smoke Chicken, Duck, Pork, Fish(腊味合蒸)

Fish Fillet with Vegetables(生熘鱼片)

Beijing cuisine(北京菜)

Beijing Roast Duck(北京烤鸭)

Instant-boiled Mutton(涮羊肉)

Shanghai cuisine(上海菜)

Chicken Wings & Legs Braised in Brown Sauce(贵妃鸡)

Duck Stuffed with Eight-treasures(八宝鸭)

Reading

Chinese Cuisine

The Chinese cuisine is subdivided into many schools with their local flavors. Among them are the most popular and well-known four schools—Beijing cuisine, Cantonese cuisine, Sichuan cuisine, and Shanghai cuisine.

Beijing Cuisine

Although these dishes are referred to as Beijing dishes, they are said to consist mainly of Shandong dishes (from Shandong Province). Most have a high calorie value answering the demands

of the cold northern climate. Beijing food is famous for its **refined ingredients and varies with the seasonings**. The **condiments** used are sugar, **vinegar**, spices, brown paste, etc. The chefs are good at making precious sea food and lay stress on making good soup. Well-known Beijing dishes include Whole Roast Duck or 'Peking Duck', Shuan Yang Rou(slices of lamb which you dip in boiling water and then coat with a do-it-yourself sauce), roast lamb and crab.

refined [rɪ'faɪnd] adj. 精炼［制］的
condiment ['kɒndɪmənt] n. 佐料，调味品
vinegar ['vɪnɪɡə] n. 醋
extravagant [ɪks'trævəɡənt] adj. 奢侈的
gourmet ['ɡʊəmeɪ] n. 美食家
pungent ['pʌndʒənt] adj. 辣的；(气味等的)刺激性的，刺鼻的

Cantonese Cuisine

In ancient times, there was a saying in China, 'To be born in Suzhou; to live in Hangzhou; to be fed in Canton'. It is also said that the people of Beijing are lovers of leisure pursuits; the Shanghainese are **extravagant** in dress; and the Cantonese are **gourmets**. Indeed, Guangdong may be said to have a greater variety of food than any other places in the world.

Cantonese food is also called the Yue food. Cantonese food features a wide range of ingredients. Its cuisine lays emphasis on deep frying, stewing, baking and especially on the color of the dishes. Dishes cooked in this way are crisp, light, refreshing and tasty, etc.

Sichuan Cuisine

Sichuan Province is a mountainous district in the center of China. The ingredients of its dishes are mainly mountain produce and river fish simply because the region has no sea coast. One of the reasons for its fine cooking could be the fact that skillful chefs were taken to the district by high Chinese government officials sent  to govern Sichuan towards the end of the feudal dynasties during the Yuan, Ming and Qing periods. Most of these chefs settled in Sichuan and developed new cooking styles based on the Beijing cuisine. They used ingredients of the district and adapted the dishes to local taste. Vegetables are used more than fish. The main condiments are generally bean paste and pickled pepper. Sichuan dishes are distinguished for being 'spicy and hot'. Their uniquely hot, **pungent** flavor is created by a mixture of spices and condiments, including red pepper, garlic and ginger.

Shanghai Cuisine

Shanghai dishes feature fresh fish and sea food dishes. The main cooking methods are: stewing with soy sauce, steaming, quick saute, braising, roasting, etc. Shanghai dishes are oily, tasty, sweet and colorful. Shanghai crabs are one of the greatest specialities. Crabs are in season from November through December. The locals claim that Shanghai crabs are not only larger than those of Beijing but are the tastiest in the entire country.

Speaking

Dialogue A (S: service, G: guest)

S: Good afternoon. Chinese Restaurant, Jessise Speaking. How may I help you?

G: What are your restaurant hours?

S: We open at 5 pm and we close at 9:30 pm, sir.

G: Is there a minimum charge and any service charge for the table?

S: Yes. The minimum charge is 100 *yuan* per person, and plus 10% service charge. But a 10% discount will be offered to those holding a VIP card issued by our restaurant.

G: I have a VIP card. Will I still be charged for liquors brought in?

S: Yes. All liquors brought in will be subject to 30% service charge based on the market price of the liquor.

G: OK, I see. I'd like to make a reservation for tonight.

S: How many people are there in your party?

G: Six.

S: What time would you need the table?

G: Around 7:00 pm.

S: Would you like to make the reservation for a private room or for a table in the hall?

G: A private room. And is there a private toilet room provided with the room?

S: Yes, it is. Would you please tell me your name and room number?

G: Will Black in Room 1212.

S: Thank you, Mr. Black. I will reserve a private room for you.

Dialogue B (W: waiter, G: guest)

W: Good evening, sir. Please have a cup of tea. Here is the menu. Take your time and I will return in a few minutes to take your order.

G: Thank you.

Unit 12 In Chinese Restaurant

W: May I take your order now, sir?

G: It's my first time to come to Chinese Restaurant. Do you have any recommendations?

W: Chinese food is divided into many schools with their local flavors. The most popular are Sichuan food, Cantonese food, and Beijing food. We have a variety of Chinese food and wine at your choice.

G: I'd like to taste a selection of Cantonese food.

W: Cantonese food is light and sweet. Fried pork in sweet and sour sauce is traditional Cantonese food.

G: That's fine. I have eaten it in Chinatown. Could you recommend any Beijing dishes for me?

W: Why not try 'Beijing roast duck'? Wrap it in the pancake with the spring onion and the sweet bean sauce. You will find the taste's better.

G: OK, I will take it. How about Sichuan food?

W: Sichuan food is spicy and hot.

G: Oh, I don't like it.

W: May I recommend Braised Prawns for you?

G: OK. Give one.

W: Would you like to try some Chinese wine?

G: Two bottles of Qingdao beer.

W: Fried Pork in Sweet and Sour Sauce, Beijing Roast Duck, Braised Prawns and two bottles of Qingdao beer. Is that right?

G: Yes, that's right. Thank you.

W: Your order will be ready soon.

Dialogue C (W: waiter, G: guest)

W: Good evening, madam and sir. Are all the guests here, now?

G1: Yes, we will have our dinner now. We will experience the fantastic feeling of Chinese banquet.

W: What kind of drinks would you prefer?

G1: A bottle of red wine, a bottle of Wu Liang Ye. And a litre of fresh watermelon juice for the children.

W: I will have them served right away.

(After a minute)

W: This is our deluxe cold dish combination with bean curd, duck's feet and sea food.

G2: Oh, it looks nice, doesn't it?

W: Now you will have Shark's Fin with Crab Meat.

G3: Wonderful.

W: Here is the Grilled Pigeon. It's the house specialty.

G4: I love it.

W: The Sauteed Prawns is ready. Can I serve it now?

G5: Why not? Well, the menu says we will have another four dishes, I am nearly full.

W: The last is rice, with vegetables and meat cubes, please take your time.

G: They all taste good.

W: We hope you have enjoyed your dinner. Thank you.

Dialogue D (W: waiter, G: guest)

W: Good afternoon, sir. Welcome to Chinese Restaurant. This is the menu. Have a look at it.

G: What can I drink here?

W: Here is the wine list. Beer and Chinese white wine are all populars in China.

G: What is the difference about Mao Tai and Wu Liang Ye?

W: They are all the best liquors in China. I recommend you Wu Liang Ye. It's very strong and it smells better.

G: Really? I'd like to try it. One bottle please. How about beer?

W: Qingdao beer is very famous. But why not try Snow beer? It's the local beer.

G: OK. Six bottles, please?

W: Would you want some tea? China is the homeland of tea. There are varieties of tea in China. The most famous is green tea.

G: I've never tasted that. By the way, is there any black tea in China?

W: Yes. The most popular black tea is Oolong. It can help people lose weight, but green tea is the wisest choice especially in summer.

G: What is the jasmine tea?

W: It's a kind of green tea with the smell of jasmine.

G: Jasmine tea, please.

W: One bottle of Wu Liang Ye, six bottles of Snow beer and one pot of jasmine tea. Your order will be served in a minute.

Unit 12　In Chinese Restaurant

🎧 Functional Sentences

* Where would you like to sit? 您愿意坐在哪儿?
* Any chance of a table by the window? 有没有可能订到靠近窗子的桌位?
* I'm sorry. The window tables have all been taken.
  很抱歉,靠窗户的桌子都有人了。
* We will have you seated as soon as we get a free table. 有空座就请您入座。
* Would you please wait in the lounge for about ten minutes?
  请在休息室等待 10 分钟?
* Sorry to have kept you waiting. 很抱歉让您久等。
* Since we have a long waiting list, we would appreciate receiving your call if you are unable to come. 因为还有很多客人需要订座,如果不能来的话请电话通知。
* What kind of cuisine do you serve in your restaurant? 你们餐厅有什么菜系?
* Cantonese food is light while Shandong food is heavy.
  粤菜清淡,山东菜味重香浓。
* Sir, your dish will take 20 minutes to prepare. While waiting, would you like anything to drink? 先生,您的菜需要 20 分钟。等菜的时候,您要喝点什么吗?
* What about the Boiled Fish with Pickled Cabbage and Chili Sauce and the Spicy Sichuan Bean Curd? 酸菜鱼和四川麻辣豆腐怎么样?
* This dish looks good, smells good, and tastes good. 这道菜色、香、味俱全。
* He wants something low-salt and low-fat. 他想吃些低盐低脂肪的食物。
* This food is best eaten hot. Please enjoy your meal.
  这道菜趁热吃最好。请慢慢享用。
* I'm afraid this is not the dish I ordered. 恐怕这不是我点的菜。
* I'll check with the chef right now. 我这就去跟厨师核对一下。
* I do apologize for our mistake. 我为我们的错误表示歉意。
* We have been sitting at the table for a quarter, but the dishes we ordered haven't been served. 我们已经等了一刻钟了,但是我们点的菜还没上。
* All the drinks are on the consumption basis. 所有酒水都算在消费内。
* How would you like us to arrange the tables? 您想我们怎么摆桌子呢?
* Could you fax us the menu with the name of the banquet room?
  你能给我们发份传真,把菜单及宴会厅的名字写在上面吗?

* Everything will be ready in advance. 我们会提前准备好一切的。
* We look forward to serving you tomorrow evening. 我们期待明晚您的光临。
* A Chinese dinner usually starts with an assorted cold dish. It can be mixed seafood, poultry or vegetables. Then comes the shark's fin soup. 中式宴会通常以什锦拼盘为第一道菜。什锦拼盘可以和海鲜类、家禽类或素菜类混合,然后是鱼翅汤。
* Banquet reception is very important for success of a banquet, because it gives the guests the first impression of the whole experience. 宴会接待是成功举办宴会的非常重要的因素,因为它会给客人留下对宴会整体的第一印象。
* The moon cake is a kind of baked cake made with fillings of nuts, fruits, meat or other stuffing. 月饼是一种用果仁、水果、肉或者其他填料做馅烤制出的糕饼。

 Writing

Task 1

Complaint Letters

客人到餐厅就餐,有时会对餐厅的菜肴及服务表示不满,事后会写信投诉餐厅。收到投诉信后,通常由餐厅经理回信,以示重视。写回信时,要表示真诚的道歉,必要时也可作一些解释,以求得客人谅解,同时要感谢客人对餐厅工作的支持并欢迎他再次光临。

以下是餐饮部经理王林先生接到的客人投诉信。

Feb. 5, 2010

Dear Sir,

I must complain in writing about the service at your restaurant last month. I dined at your restaurant on 21st Jan. 2010 in a group of 12 people from overseas at 7:00 pm. I could tell that when we started, things would be difficult as the restaurant had a couple of other groups and was reasonably busy. The issues were as follows:

Staff—there was not enough staff for the size of the restaurant and we had to wait too long for everything. At times staff stood behind the bar, chatting, and did not pay attention to the customers at all.

Food—overall food quality was good and tasty but timing terrible—we waited so long for starters.

To be honest this restaurant just does not have a good system or staff for the size of the place. It is not inexpensive and would have expected better. This was one of my worst experiences I have had.

I do not usually complain but, as an old customer, I'm sure you will be interested in my comments.

Yours faithfully,
Bill Smith

以下是王林经理的回信。

Feb. 10, 2010

Dear Mr. Smith,

Shenyang Hotel is always interested in hearing the comments from its guests and we are glad that you have written to us.

I am extremely sorry that you found the service provided by our staff was not up to our usual standard. I do apologize for this and will make enquiries about it.

You took your holiday last month which was our busiest month. The service arrangement for you was not very attractive. However, I regret that you had slow service at dinner.

I hope we will continue to receive your comments and that if you have any complaint, you will inform my staff immediately so that we can deal with the problem there.

Yours sincerely,
Wanglin
Manager
Food & Beverage Dept.
Shenyang Hotel

Exercise:

请你就以下内容给 Bill Brown 写一封回信。

Mr. Bill Brown has complained about the standard of service in the Holiday Restaurant. He says that he had to wait thirty minutes for his table, that the service was slow, and that the food was not very good.

Now write a letter of reply to the complaint received by the restaurant.

Exercises

一、Complete the following dialogues.

Dialogue 1 (W: waiter, G: guest)

W: Good evening, sir and madam. _____.

G: Good evening. A table for four, please.

W: _____?

G: I don't think we have.

W: _____. Would you please wait in the lounge for about 10 minutes?

G: OK.

W: Sorry to have kept you waiting. _____? By the window or further back?

G: We would like a table by the window so that we can enjoy the view of the lake.

W: This way, please. _____?

G: That's fine.

W: Here is the menu. Take your time.

G: Thank you.

Dialogue 2 (W: waiter, G: guest)

G: Can I have the bill, please?

W: Yes, sir. I hope you have enjoyed your dinner.

G: The food is quite good. How much is that?

W: RMB 680 in all, sir. _____?

G: Do you accept credit cards?

W: Yes, we accept American Express, Visa, Master and Diner's Club.

G: That's good. Mine is Visa.

W: _____?

G: Here you are.

W: Thank you. Sorry, sir. The card is expired. _____?

G: You may try this one.

W: _____?

G: Of course.

W: Here are the bill and the receipt. Have a nice day.

二、**Complete the dialogue with the Chinese prompts.**

W: 晚上好,女士、先生们。一张六人桌?请这边走。

G: 谢谢。

W: 需要喝点什么吗?

G: 请给我两瓶啤酒,四听可乐。

W：请问点菜吗？

G：你有什么推荐？

W：如果您喜欢辣的，何不试试著名的四川菜——麻婆豆腐。

G：好吧。还有什么别的辣菜适合我们？

W：四川牛柳丝好吗？

G：好极了！就这样。给我一份北京烤鸭好么？

W：好的，先生。需要米饭和汤吗？

G：玉米羹和两份扬州炒饭。

W：马上为您上菜。

三、Put the following into English.

1. 请替我订一张带转盘的八人桌子。

2. 我一会儿就给您上菜。

3. 粤菜比较清淡；而川菜呢，辛辣又刺激。

4. 我想要一份宫保鸡丁，能快点上菜吗？

5. 这是您点的回锅肉、松鼠鳜鱼和麻婆豆腐。

6. 今天有葱油饼和春卷。

7. 这是全部的菜。如果您还想要加菜，请叫我。

8. 您想订中式、西式、日式还是韩式菜肴？

9. 您打算每位消费多少？

10. 宴会场地是什么样的？室内还是室外的？

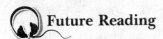

Starwood Hotels

Starwood is one of major international hotel chains with brands and products that range from upscale luxury hotels to good quality three-and four-star hotels that include a number under its Sheraton and Four Points by Sheraton brands. The company owns or manages 871 properties and offers 265,500 rooms in more than 100 countries. In 2006 the asset value of the company was US＄9,280 million. Its total revenue was a fraction under US＄6,000 million and, according to its 2006 Accounts, its hotels were valued at over US＄2 billion.

Starwood is a relatively new name in the hotel industry, having a history of just over a decade, being formed by Barry Sternlicht from a nearly bankrupt real estate investment trust with a pure USA base of interests. Its leading flagship brand names include W. Westin, Sheraton and St. Regis. Most of these hotels are located in urban areas, with some emphasis on central business districts, and one advantage of such sites is that they pose high level barriers to entry to potential competitors because of high construction costs, or high costs of purchase due to usually high occupancy rates caused by that location. In addition, of course, its brands, especially that of the Sheraton, are widely known and respected. Its move from  being a real estate investment company, Starwood Capital (formed in 1991 by Sternlicht) to being a hotel company was initially motivated by tax considerations and the wish to take advantage of what were termed 'grand-fathered tax breaks'. These had been outlawed in the USA, but Sternlicht was able to access them through the purchase of a rare form of Real Estate Investment Trust (what was called a pair-shared REIT), namely Hotel Investors Trust. In 1994 it purchased the Westin Hotel Company from the Aoki Corporation of Japan. In 1998 it added the Sheraton portfolio of Sheraton, Four Points by Sheraton and The Luxury Collection from ITT Sheraton. Its own, new brand, "W" was launched in 1999 with the objective of being 'fun, hip, and exciting' that 'marries boutique hotel flair with the quality and functionality of larger brand hotels'. Encouraged by this success, in September 2005 a new brand aimed at the business segment of the market was launched, namely Aloft. The objective is to have 500 Aloft hotels worldwide by 2012. In the same year the group purchased the chain of Le Meridien hotels, thereby permitting a larger presence in Europe.

In 2004 Barry Sternlicht stepped down as CEO of the company, and under his successor, Steven J. Heyer, the company began a new direction of selling properties with the purpose of increasingly becoming a management and franchisor for current and future brands. This new direction was halted as increasing criticisms and concerns began to be voiced, and in April 2007 Heyer left the company officially due to concerns about his management style. Barry Duncan, chair of the board then took the role of acting CEO. Nonetheless, in spite of these problems associated with individuals amongst the executives and directors, the consensus in the business and the hospitality press remained that the group was well positioned in the hotel industry. However, in 2007 the company is still perceived by some as a target for a leveraged buyout by a private equity company, which would be part of a current corporate trend that is affecting the business world generally including the hotel industry. For example, in March 2007 Hilton sold its Scandic chain to Swedish buyout firm EGT and Four Seasons Hotels Inc. was taken into private hands for US $3.27 billion by a group that included Microsoft Chair Bill Gates and Saudi Prince Alwaleed Bin Talal. Subsequently of course, Hilton was then purchased by Blackstones.

Certainly the Starwood group has a proven financial record. In the years 2004, 2005 and 2006 its net income has increased with the figures being US $395 million, US $422 million and US $1.04 billion respectively.

Vocabulary

Unit 1 Giving Travel Information

destination [ˌdestɪˈneɪʃn] *n.* 目的地,终点

subscribe [səbˈskraɪb] *vi.* (to)订阅,订购

notification [ˌnəʊtɪfɪˈkeɪʃn] *n.* 通知

medical evacuation [ɪˌvækjʊˈeɪʃn] *n.* 医疗救助

participate [pɑːˈtɪsɪpeɪt] *vi.* 参加,参与

embassy [ˈembəsɪ] *n.* 大使馆

high commission 高级专员

consulate [ˈkɒnsjʊlɪt] *n.* 领事馆

emergency [ɪˈmɜːdʒənsɪ] *n.* 紧急情况,非常时刻

override [ˌəʊvəˈraɪd] *vt.* 优先于

harsh [hɑːʃ] *adj.* 严厉(酷)的

transit [ˈtrænsɪt] *n.* 过境;通过,中转

vaccination [ˌvæksɪˈneɪʃn] *n.* 疫苗接种

precaution [prɪˈkɔːʃn] *n.* 预防

validity [vəˈlɪdɪtɪ] *n.* 有效期

itinerary [aɪˈtɪnərərɪ] *n.* 行程表,旅行路线

dual [ˈdjuːəl] *adj.* 双(重)的

in bulk 大量,大批

access to 接近

escorted tours 全程陪同旅游

regimentation [ˌredʒɪmenˈteɪʃn] *n.* 严格控制

superficial [ˌsuːpəˈfɪʃəl] *adj.* 肤浅的,表面的

gear [gɪə] *vt.* (to)使适合

denominator [dɪˈnɒmɪneɪtə] *n.* 平均水平

get stuck with 无法摆脱,困于

incompatible [ˌɪnkəmˈpætəbəl] *adj.* 不相容的

package tour 包价旅行（由旅行社安排一切的一揽子旅游）
penalty ['penltɪ] n. 惩罚，罚款
universal [ˌjuːnɪ'vɜːsəl] adj. 普遍的
phenomena [fɪ'nɒmɪnə] n. (pl.) 现象
rigid ['rɪdʒɪd] adj. 严格的，死板的
compact [kəm'pækt] adj. 紧凑的
linger ['lɪŋɡə] vi. 逗留，留恋徘徊
inhale [ɪn'heɪl] v. 吸入（气体等）
budget ['bʌdʒɪt] n. 预算

Unit 2 At the Airport

verify ['verɪfaɪ] vt. 核实，查对
visible ['vɪzəbl] adj. 看得见的，明显的
procedure [prə'siːdʒə] n. 程序，手续，步骤
logo ['ləʊɡəʊ] n. （企业、公司等的）专用标识
domestic [də'mestɪk] adj. 国内的
depart [dɪ'pɑːt] vi. 离开，出发
regulation [ˌreɡju'leɪʃn] n. 规章，规则
comply [kəm'plaɪ] vi. (with) 遵从，依从，服从
customs ['kʌstəmz] adj. 海关的
embarkation [ˌembɑː'keɪʃn] n. 乘船，搭机
currency ['kʌrənsɪ] n. 货币
diplomat ['dɪpləmæt] n. 外交官，外交家
Customs declaration form 海关申报表
souvenir [ˌsuːvə'nɪə] n. 纪念品，纪念物
duty ['djuːtɪ] n. 税；关税
scale [skeɪl] n. 磅秤
claim baggage 提取行李

Unit 3 Local Tour Guide Service

representative [ˌreprɪ'zentətɪv] n. 代表
professional [prə'feʃnl] adj. 职业的，专业的
vitally ['vaɪtəlɪ] adv. 极其重要地
emotional [ɪ'məʊʃənl] adj. 令人动情的；易动感情的

proficient [prəˈfɪʃənt] adj. 熟练的,精通的
archeology [ˌɑːkɪˈɒlədʒɪ] n. 考古学,古物
architecture [ˈɑːkɪtektʃə] n. 建筑学(术、业)
folklore [ˈfəʊklɔː] n. 民俗学,民间传说
resolve [rɪˈzɒlv] vt. 解决(答)
conflict [ˈkɒnflɪkt] n. 冲突,争论
mild [maɪld] adj. 温和的,温柔的
passionate [ˈpæʃənɪt] adj. 充满激情的
courageous [kəˈreɪdʒəs] adj. 勇敢的;无畏的
persevering [ˌpɜːsɪˈvɪərɪŋ] adj. 坚忍不拔的
ideology [ˌaɪdɪˈɒlədʒɪ] n. 思想(体系),思想意识
upright [ˈʌpraɪt] adj. 正直的
corruption [kəˈrʌpʃn] n. 腐化;贪污
prudent [ˈpruːdənt] adj. 审慎的,小心谨慎的
diligent [ˈdɪlɪdʒənt] adj. 勤勉的,勤奋的
magnificent [mæɡˈnɪfɪsənt] adj. 壮丽的,宏伟的
thrive [θraɪv] vi. 兴旺,繁荣
ratify [ˈrætɪfaɪ] vt. 正式批准
feast [fiːst] v. 款待,享受
unparalleled [ʌnˈpærəleld] adj. 无比的
intrigue [ɪnˈtriːɡ] vt. 激起兴趣,迷住
abundance [əˈbʌndəns] n. 大量,丰富,充足
down garment 羽绒服
vitality [vaɪˈtælɪtɪ] n. 活力;生命力
authentic [ɔːˈθentɪk] adj. 真的,真正的
acquainted [əˈkweɪntɪd] adj. 熟悉的,认识的
matchless [ˈmætʃləs] adj. 无敌的,无比的
vigor [ˈvɪɡə] n. 活力
acrobatics [ˌækrəˈbætɪks] n. 杂技
martial [ˈmɑːʃəl] adj. 军事的;战争的
enchantment [ɪnˈtʃɑːntmənt] n. 着魔,喜悦
encounter [ɪnˈkaʊntə] vt. 遇到
meditate [ˈmedɪteɪt] vi. 沉思
precaution [prɪˈkɔːʃn] n. 预防,防备,警惕

pickpocket ['pɪkpɒkɪt] n. 扒手
instinct ['ɪnstɪŋkt] n. 本能,直觉;生性,天性
charity ['tʃærɪtɪ] n. [pl.] 慈善团体
street vendor 街头小贩
gorgeous ['gɔːrdʒəs] adj. 华丽的;灿烂的
bund [bʌnd] n. 外滩
explicit [ɪkˈsplɪsɪt] adj. 详尽的;明确的;清楚的
cruise [kruːz] v. 巡游;巡航

Unit 4 Shopping

bargain ['bɑːgən] vi. 讨价还价
porcelain ['pɔːsəlɪn] n. 瓷器
essential [ɪˈsenʃ(ə)l] adj. 必需的;基本的
necessity [nəˈsesətɪ] n. 必需品
preserve [prɪˈzɜːv] vi. 做蜜饯,做果酱,做罐头
handicraft ['hændɪkrɑːft] n. 手工艺品
commodity [kəˈmɒdɪtɪ] n. [pl.] 日用品;商品
aspect ['æspekt] n. 方面;情况
calculate ['kælkjʊleɪt] vt. 计算
appeal to 吸引
overall ['əʊvərɔːl] adv. 总的来说;大体上
irritable ['ɪrɪtəbl] adj. 易怒的,性急的
curved [kɜːvd] adj. 弯曲的
angle ['æŋgl] v. 转向或弯曲成一角度
swarm [swɔːm] v. 云集
sandalwood ['sændəlwʊd] n. 檀香木,檀香木色
calligraphy [kəˈlɪgrəfɪ] n. 笔迹,书法
miniature ['mɪnətʃə] n. 缩小模型,缩微复制品

Unit 5 Entertainment

fade [feɪd] vi. 渐渐消失
deem [diːm] vt. 认为
stilt [stɪlt] n. 高跷
glutinous ['gluːtɪnəs] adj. 黏性的

worship ['wɜːʃɪp] vt. 崇拜，尊敬
mugwort ['mʌgwɜːt] n. 艾蒿
satchel ['sætʃəl] n. 书包，小背包
constellation [ˌkɒnstə'leɪʃn] n. 星座；荟萃
chrysanthemum [krɪ'sænθəməm] n. 菊；菊花
exquisite ['ekskwɪzɪt] adj. 精美的
lustrous ['lʌstrəs] adj. 光泽的
lacquer ['lækə] n. 漆，天然漆；漆器
ceramic [sɪ'ræmɪk] n. [pl.] 陶瓷器
embroidery [ɪm'brɔɪdərɪ] n. 刺绣，刺绣品
utensil [juː'tensəl] n. 器皿，器具
ornamental [ˌɔːnə'mentl] adj. 装饰的
refined [rɪ'faɪnd] adj. 精炼[制]的
polish ['pɒlɪʃ] vt. 磨光，擦亮
embed [ɪm'bed] vt. 把……嵌(埋、插)入
contemporary [kən'temprərɪ] adj. 当代的
reputation [ˌrepju'teɪʃn] n. 名气，名声，名誉
essence ['esəns] n. 精髓，精华
oriental [ˌɔːrɪ'entl] adj. 东方的，东方文化的
texture ['tekstʃə] n. 质地
luster ['lʌstə] n. 光辉
masterpiece ['mɑːstəpiːs] n. 杰作
outstanding [aʊt'stændɪŋ] adj. 突(杰)出的
sculpt [skʌlpt] v. 雕刻
adroit [ə'drɔɪt] adj. 灵巧的
grotto ['grɒtəʊ] n. 岩穴；洞室
immortal [ɪ'mɔːtl] adj. 不朽的
originate [ə'rɪdʒɪneɪt] vi. 起源于，来自
freestanding [ˌfriː'stændɪŋ] adj. 独立式的
relief [rɪ'liːf] n. 浮雕
bronze [brɒnz] n. 青铜；青铜制品
sophisticated [sə'fɪstɪkeɪtɪd] adj. 老练的；精密的
imposing [ɪm'pəʊzɪŋ] adj. 壮丽的，雄伟的
cloisonné [klwɑː'zʊneɪ] n. 景泰蓝

Vocabulary

filigree [ˈfɪlɪgriː] n. 金银丝做的工艺品
filature [ˈfɪlətʃə] n. 缫丝，纺丝
brocade [brəˈkeɪd] n. 锦缎，织锦
Persia [ˈpɜːʃə] n. 波斯［现称伊朗］
troupe [truːp] n. 歌唱团，剧团
stage [steɪdʒ] vt. 上演；举办
acclaim [əˈkleɪm] n. 称赞，欢迎
synthesize [ˈsɪnθɪsaɪz] vt. 综合
stereotyped [ˈsterɪətaɪpt] adj. 固定不变的
evaluate [ɪˈvæljʊeɪt] vt. 评估，评价
filial [ˈfɪlɪəl] adj. 孝顺的
obedience [əˈbiːdjəns] n. 顺从
chastity [ˈtʃæstɪtɪ] n. 贞节，纯洁
virginity [vəˈdʒɪnɪtɪ] n. 处女性；童贞；纯洁
code [kəʊd] n. 准则
discard [dɪsˈkɑːd] vt. 丢弃，抛弃
dross [drɒs] n. 浮渣，糟粕
virtue [ˈvɜːtʃuː] n. 美德
laud [lɔːd] vt. 赞美
The Butterfly Lovers《梁山伯与祝英台》
Fifteen Strings of Coins《十五弦硬币》
redress [rɪˈdres] vt. 纠正
elaborate [ɪˈlæbərət, -reɪt] adj. 详尽的；复杂的
costume [ˈkɒstjuːm] n. （流行的）服饰；戏装
prop [prɒp] n. 道具
heritage [ˈherɪtɪdʒ] n. 遗产，继承物，传统
pagoda [pəˈgəʊdə] n. 塔，宝塔
stack [stæk] vt. 堆，摞
incredible [ɪnˈkredəbl] adj. 不可信的；不可思议的
applaud [əˈplɔːd] vt. 向……鼓掌
stabilize [ˈsteɪbəlaɪz] v. （使）稳定，（使）稳固
feat [fiːt] n. 技艺
mezzanine [ˈmezəniːn] n. 中层楼（底楼与二楼之间）
slack [slæk] n. 宽松的裤子，便裤

143

Unit 6　Handling Problems and Emergencies

fraudulent ['frɔːdjələnt] adj. 欺诈的,不诚实的
tampering ['tæmpə] vi. 干预,损害　vt. 篡改
impound [ɪm'paʊnd] vt. 扣押
deportation [ˌdiːpɔː'teɪʃn] n. 驱逐出境
obstruct [əb'strʌkt] vt. 阻隔,妨碍,阻塞
pinch [pɪntʃ] vt. 捏,拧,掐,挤压
exhale [eks'heɪl] vt. 呼气,发出,散发
vomit ['vɒmɪt] vt. 吐出,呕吐
suffocate ['sʌfəkeɪt] vt. 使窒息,噎住;闷熄
arterial [ɑː'tɪəriəl] adj. 动脉的,脉络状的
hypothermia [ˌhaɪpə'θɜːmiə] n. 低体温
torso ['tɔːsəʊ] n. 躯干
cardiac ['kɑːdiæk] n. 心脏病患者;强心剂;健胃药　adj. 心脏的;(胃的)贲门的
armpit ['ɑːmpɪt] n. 腋窝
tub [tʌb] n. 桶,浴盆
fracture ['fræktʃə] n. 破碎,骨折
splint [splɪnt] vt. 用夹板固定
accredit [ə'kredɪt] vt. 信托,委派
incorporat [ɪn'kɔːpəreɪt] vt. (into)吸收;合并
offset ['ɒfset] n. 抵消
patron ['peɪtrən] n. 赞助人;顾客;保护人
seminar ['semɪnɑː] 研讨班;研讨会
encounter [ɪn'kaʊntə] vt. 遇见,邂逅
witness ['wɪtnɪs] vt. 目击,证明
donate ['dəʊneɪt] vt. 捐赠
subtle ['sʌtl] adj. 微妙的
irreversible [ˌɪrɪ'vɜːsəbl] adj. 不能倒逆的;不能翻转的

Unit 7　Room Reservation

hospitality industry 酒店行业
enterprise ['entəpraɪz] n. 企业
lodging ['lɒdʒɪŋ] n. 寄宿

institutional food and beverage services 大众餐饮业服务机构

cater ['keɪtə] vt. 迎合

stand apart 自成一家

accommodation [əˌkɒməˈdeɪʃn] n. 住处

property ['prɒpəti] n. 功能

be composed of 由……组成

oriented ['ɔːrientɪd] v. 以……为目的

segment ['segmənt] v. 分割成部分

retail store 零售商店

motel [məʊˈtel] n. 汽车旅馆

suite [swiːt] hotel 套间酒店,指的是酒店的所有房间都是套房,除卧室还有厨房、会客室等

affiliation [əˌfɪliˈeɪʃn] n. 联系,从属关系

transient ['trænzɪənt] adj. 短暂的

residential relocation 居住空间重置

integral ['ɪntɪɡrəl] adj. 主要的

standard room 标准间

junior suite 简单套房

deluxe [dəˈlʌks] suite 豪华套房

president suite 总统套房

settle one's account 结账

guarantee [ˌɡærənˈtiː] vt. 保证

expiry date 有效期限

official release time 官方发布的时间

accurately ['ækjərətli] adv. 正确地,精确地

Unit 8 Reception Service

relevant ['relɪvənt] adj. 有关的

arrival list 到达客人名单

in advance 预先,事先

status ['steɪtəs] n. 情形,状态

allocate ['æləkeɪt] vt. 分配

folio ['fəʊliəʊ] n. 客人的账户

registration form 登记表

clarify [ˈklærɪfaɪ] vt. 澄清
monitor [ˈmɒnɪtə] vt. 监视
undergo [ˌʌndəˈɡəʊ] vt. 经历
be convinced of 确信
amenity [əˈmiːnətɪ] n. 方便设施
rollaway bed 折叠床
crib [krɪb] n. 有围栏的童床
proof [pruːf] n. 证据,证明
valid [ˈvælɪd] adj. 有效的
assurance [əˈʃʊərəns] n. 信心;保证
premise [ˈpremɪs] n. 前提;假定
requisite [ˈrekwɪzɪt] adj. 需要的;必要的
enhance [ɪnˈhɑːns] vt. 提高,增加,加强
capture [ˈkæptʃə] vt. 俘虏,捕获;夺得
deferred payment 推迟付款
debit card 借记卡
smart card 智能卡;房卡
alternative [ɔːlˈtɜːnətɪv] adj. 可用以代替其他事物的
outset [ˈaʊtset] n. 开始,开端
escort [ˈeskɔːt] vt. 护送,护卫
loose-leaf adj. 活页式的
accessible [əkˈsesəbl] adj. 容易取得的
spot [spɒt] vt. 认出
suspect [ˈsʌspekt] adj. 可疑的
compile [kəmˈpaɪl] vt. 汇编,编制
conjunction [kənˈdʒʌŋkʃn] n. 联合
obnoxious [əbˈnɒkʃəs] adj. 可憎的
abusive [əˈbjuːsɪv] adj. 辱骂的
fixture [ˈfɪkstʃə] n. [pl.] 固定装置
fitting [ˈfɪtɪŋ] n. [pl.] 设备;家具
trickster [ˈtrɪkstə] n. 骗子;耍诡计的人
obligation [ˌɒblɪˈɡeɪʃn] n. 义务,责任
solvency [ˈsɒlvənsɪ] n. 还债能力
notoriously [nəʊˈtɔːrɪəslɪ] adv. 恶名昭彰地

hassle ['hæsəl] n. 激烈的辩论
aggravation [ˌægrə'veɪʃn] n. 加重,恶化
bona fide [ˌbəʊnə'faɪdɪ] adj. 真实(的)

Unit 9　In-house Service

rate [reɪt] n. 房价
timely ['taɪmlɪ] adj. 及时的
status ['steɪtəs] n. 情形,状况
register ['redʒɪstə] vt. 登记
vacant ['veɪkənt] adj. 空着的;空缺的
subsequent ['sʌbsɪkwənt] adj. 随后的,后来的
correspondence [ˌkɒrə'spɒndəns] n. 信件
amendment [ə'mendmənt] n. 修正,改进
porter ['pɔːtə] n. 搬运工人;看门人
occupancy ['ɒkjəpənsɪ] n. 占有,使用;居住
coordinate [kəʊ'ɔːdɪneɪt] vt. 调节,协调
concierge [ˌkɔːnsɪ'eəʒ] n. [法]门卫;接待员
resolve [rɪ'zɒlv] vt. 解决(答);
security [sɪ'kjʊərɪtɪ] n. 安全,保障
issue ['ɪʃuː, 'ɪsjuː] n. 问题
interface ['ɪntəfeɪs] v. 连接　n. 接口;交界面
revenue ['revɪnjuː] n. (大宗的)收入(益);税收
posting ['pəʊstɪŋ] n. 过账;记账;登账
auditing ['ɔːdɪtɪŋ] n. 审计;查账;决算
lounge [laʊndʒ] n. 休息室,娱乐室
outlet ['aʊtlet] n. 部门
exceed [ɪk'siːd] vt. 超过,越出
periodically [ˌpɪərɪ'ɒdɪkəlɪ] adv. 定期地
routine [ruː'tiːn] n. 例行公事,惯例
verification [ˌverɪfɪ'keɪʃn] n. 证实;验证
discrepancy [dɪs'krepənsɪ] n. 不符合(之处),不一致(之处)

Unit 10　Check-out Service

post outstanding charges 把客人在酒店每个部门的消费都记在客账上

verify ['verɪfaɪ] vt. 核实,查对

update [ˌʌp'deɪt] vt. 更新

vacate [veɪ'keɪt] v. 空出

accurate ['ækjʊrɪt] adj. 准确的

anticipate [æn'tɪsɪpeɪt] vt. 预期(料),期望

clientele [ˌkliːən'tel] n. 顾客,常客

profile ['prəʊfaɪl] n. 侧面;轮廓

prior to 在……之前

apply pre-established direct billing instructions 申请预先制定的直接结算指令

late charge 最新消费

incur [ɪn'kɜː] vt. 招致,遭受,引起

irritation [ˌɪrɪ'teɪʃn] n. (被)激怒

submit [səb'mɪt] vt. 呈送,提交

outstanding [aʊt'stændɪŋ] adj. 未偿还的;尚未支付的

generate ['dʒenəreɪt] vt. 生成,产生

isolate ['aɪsəleɪt] vt. 隔离

highlight ['haɪlaɪt] vt. 强调,突出

evaluate [ɪ'væljʊeɪt] vt. 评估,评价

encounter [ɪn'kaʊntə] vt. 遇到

prime [praɪm] adj. 首要的;最好的

ease [iːz] v. 缓和,解除

initiate [ɪ'nɪʃɪeɪt] vt. 开始

notify ['nəʊtɪfaɪ] vt. 通知

authorize ['ɔːθəraɪz] vt. 授权,批准

voucher ['vaʊtʃə] n. 凭单,收据

crested ['krestɪd] vt. 在……上加顶饰

deposit [dɪ'pɒzɪt] vt. 寄存

relay ['riːleɪ] vt. 传达

Unit 11　　A La Carte

guava ['gwɑːvə] n. 番石榴(生长于热带)

papaya [pə'paɪə] n. 木瓜

semi-milk 半脂牛奶

soymilk ['sɔɪmɪlk] n. 豆奶

oatmeal [ˈəʊtmiːl] *n.* 燕麦片；燕麦粥

cornmeal [ˈkɔːnmiːl] *n.* 玉米片；麦片

rice crispies, rye crispies, puff rice, wheaties, cheerios 各种麦片

croissant [ˈkrwæsɒŋ] *n.* (From *French* 法)新月形面包(用于早餐中食用)

cinnamon [ˈsɪnəmən] *n.* 肉桂

miniature [ˈmɪnɪətʃə] *adj.* 小型的，微小的

assorted [əˈsɔːtɪd] *adj.* 各种各样的

marmalade [ˈmɑːməleɪd] *n.* 酸果酱；(尤指)橙子酱

omelet [ˈɒmlɪt] *n.* 煎蛋卷，鸡蛋卷

bacon [ˈbeɪkən] *n.* 咸肉

outlet [ˈaʊtlet, -lɪt] *n.* 【商】销路，市场

haute cuisine [əʊt kwɪˈziːn] *n.* (法)高级烹饪

license [ˈlaɪsns] *vt.* 发许可证，准许

ally to [ˈælaɪ, əˈlaɪ] 与……结盟

Unit 12　In Chinese Restaurant

refined [rɪˈfaɪnd] *adj.* 精炼[制]的

condiment [ˈkɒndɪmənt] *n.* 佐料，调味品

vinegar [ˈvɪnɪgə] *n.* 醋

extravagant [ɪksˈtrævəgənt] *adj.* 奢侈的

gourmet [ˈgʊəmeɪ] *n.* 美食家

pungent [ˈpʌndʒənt] *adj.* 辣的；(气味等的)刺激性的，刺鼻的

参考答案

Unit 1　Giving Travel Information

一、**Complete the following dialogues.**

Dialogue 1

It's my pleasure

So where shall I begin my sightseeing

What do you like to do in your spare time

but I've been meaning to

That sounds like a great plan

Dialogue 2

it is my pleasure to help you

what would you suggest that I visit first

So do you have another place in mind

Tell me what interests you

I haven't had a chance to go to either of them

二、**Complete the dialogue with the Chinese prompts.**

A: Can I help you?

B: My wife and I want to go to Beijing for a tour. Can you arrange it?

A: Yes, we can arrange that.

B: I'd like to know what kind of tour your travel agency has?

A: Our travel agency provides all kinds of tours, ranging from individual tours to group package tours.

B: Excellent.

A: When do you expect to come?

B: October 8th.

A: What specific places do you wish to visit?

B: We would like to visit the Great Wall, the Imperial Palace and the Summer Palace.

A: OK.

三、**Put the following into English.**

1. Where is the tourist information?

2. Can you arrange a trip for us?

3. How are you going, by train or by plane?

4. Are all meals included in the price?

5. Is there any extra charge?

6. I've decided to go on a one-week tour of Thailand.

7. What type of visa are you applying for?

8. May I have a look at your return flight ticket?

9. Are you on a tourist visa or a business visa?

10. We will get in touch with you when your visa is ready.

Unit 2　At the Airport

一、**Complete the following dialogue.**

Yes, it is

Here you are

Is the flight on schedule

二、**Complete the dialogues with the Chinese prompts.**

Dialogue 1

A: Good morning. Your ticket and passport, please?

B: Here you are.

A: Do you have any baggage to check in?

B: Yes, one box.

A: Would you please put it on the scale?

B: OK. By the way, can you tell me how many kilos of free baggage each passenger is allowed?

A: The baggage allowance is different according to the class of your ticket. What class are you travelling?

B: First class.

A: For a first-class passenger, the free baggage allowance is forty kilos.

B: How many pieces of baggage can I carry onto the plane?

A: Passengers holding first-class tickets may carry 2 pieces within the total weight of 5 kg onto the plane.

B: If my baggage exceeds the allowance, what should I do?

A: If the checked baggage is over the allowance, we will charge you for the overweight.

B: I see. Thank you very much for your information.

A: You are welcome. Your boarding pass and baggage check, please.

B: Good-bye.

Dialogue 2

A: Excuse me, what is the easiest way to downtown?

B: There are several ways. You may take the city bus, that's the cheapest. There are also shuttle buses or limousines. The fastest way is to simply take a taxi.

A: Okay, I will take the shuttle bus. Can you tell me where to find it?

B: Just outside the gate.

Dialogue 3

A: Excuse me, where is the baggage claim area?

B: Go down this hallway and at the end, turn right.

A: Thank you. And how will I know where to find my luggage?

B: On which flight did you just arrive?

A: I was on United Airlines flight 446 from Tokyo.

B: You'll find your luggage on carousel number three.

三、**Put the following into English.**

1. Welcome to China!
2. You all need a good rest first.
3. You will have plenty of time to see all the interesting places in China.
4. Shall I help you with your luggage?
5. May I have your ticket and passport, please?
6. Which is the security check counter?
7. Where is Gate 5?
8. When will the flight begin boarding?
9. How much hand luggage am I allowed?
10. Could you show me how to fill in the declaration card?

Unit 3   Local Tour Guide Service

一、**Complete the following dialogue.**

How many days will you be visiting here

Have you ever visited our city before

I really enjoy visiting museums and art galleries

二、**Complete the dialogues with the Chinese prompts.**

Dialogue 1

A: Where should we go sightseeing today?

B: I think that some things might be best done in the morning and others in the afternoon.

A: I think that I would like to go to the beach this morning.

B: That would be a good place to start our sightseeing. We could have breakfast there.

A: I hear that there is a very nice natural history museum there.

B: Yes, it would be nice to check that out since we are so close by.

A: Where should we go in the afternoon?

B: I think that I would like to go to the amusement park. It's supposed to be quite good.

A: At the end of the day, I would love to take in the sunset at the restaurant by the park.

B: That sounds like a great idea! Let's go get a map.

Dialog 2

A: Excuse me, could you tell me how much is the ticket?

B: It is free on weekends.

A: That's great!

B: Here is a guiding plan.

A: Thank you. By the way, could I take pictures in the park?

B: Yes, why not?

A: And are there any shops in the park?

B: Yes, there are many. You can buy almost everything there.

A: I see. Thank you very much.

B: It's my pleasure.

三、Put the following into English.

1. I would like to join your tours to Shanghai on July 10th.

2. Do we have a guide who can speak English?

3. Can I have the details of the schedule of this tour?

4. We would like to take a double room with a front view.

5. There're many famous scenic spots and historical sites in Shenyang.

6. We will do our best to make your trip more enjoyable and memorable.

7. Next, I'd like to introduce something about this city.

8. Insurance is included in the package fee.

9. My wife has some motion sickness, so can the local guide prepare some medicine in case of emergency?

10. Let me introduce my team to you first.

Unit 4　Shopping

一、Complete the following dialogue.

Do you have anything in particular that you are looking for

How about the children in your family

they can vary a lot in price

That's a good idea

二、Complete the dialogues with the Chinese prompts.

Dialogue 1

A: Let's stop and look at the souvenirs at the souvenir stand.

B: What types of souvenirs were you looking for?

A: When I travel, I usually like to bring back a special necklace or clothing.

B: I always buy a lot of stuff for the kids in my family. Do you like to do that, too?

A: My family love me to take trips so they like to get the goodies I bring them.

B: What types of things do they like?

A: The little kids like little trinkets, like those little shell animals over there.

B: I feel like this stuff is kind of overpriced.

A: Some souvenir stands charge more than others, so it pays to shop around.

B: Why don't we try checking prices a little farther away from the tourist section?

A: Good idea.

Dialogue 2

A: Can I help you?

B: I'd like to buy some Chinese-style cakes. Could you recommend me some?

A: Certainly. What about the moon cake? It's typical Chinese food.

B: The moon cake? What is that?

A: The moon cake is round and looks like the full moon. That's why it's called the moon cake and the moon cake symbolizes family reunion and harmony.

B: Sounds very interesting, I'll buy some for family people.

A: All the moon cakes are generally classified into two styles: Cantonese styles and Suzhou styles.

B: What's the difference between these two styles?

A: The skin of Cantonese style cakes is soft and puffy with heavy stuffing while the skin of Suzhou style cakes is puffy filled with fragrant nuts.

B: Get me some of each.

A: OK, here you are.

三、Put the following into English.

1. Do you want to buy typical Chinese products and specialties?
2. Chinese tea is world-famous.
3. I can recommend you some famous Chinese-style pastries.
4. It has a history of more than 2,000 years.
5. Beijing Roast Duck is well-known and popular. It is agreeably fat.
6. I'd like something unique to China.
7. It is well received all over the world.
8. Suzhou silk is velvety and the color is brilliant.
9. Chinese embroidery is reputed for its high quality and design.
10. It's a famous rice wine.

Unit 5 Entertainment

一、Complete the following dialogue.

Can I help you

Are there any good seats left

what time does it begin

How many tickets do you want

Here is the money

二、Complete the dialogue with the Chinese prompts.

A: How would you like to go to a concert this evening?

B: I'd like to very much.

A: That's great.

B: Who's playing?

A: It's the National Symphony Orchestra.

B: Great! I can't wait to go to the theatre.

A: Don't worry. It will begin at 8:00 pm. Let's book some tickets first.

B: Good idea. Let's go.

三、Put the following into English.

1. How about going to a movie?

2. The film has been shown in many countries.

3. Who do you think is the best actor?

4. This movie was very touching.

5. The story is very exciting and full of suspense.

6. I guess I expected too much from the movie, so I was a bit disappointed.

7. What's your favorite kind of music?

8. There is a folk concert tomorrow evening.

9. This song is pretty old, but I love it.

10. I like country music and classical music.

11. I have no ear for music.

Unit 6 Handling Problems and Emergencies

一、Complete the following dialogues.

Dialogue 1

What's the trouble

Have you lost your passport

When did you lose it

Thank you

Dialogue 2

What's wrong with you

When did the cough begin

What color is it

Do you have a fever

二、Complete the dialogues with the Chinese prompts.

Dialogue 1

A: Excuse me, I am a stranger here. I lost my way.

B: Where do you want to go?

A: Could you show me the way to the Imperial Palace?

B: Certainly, go down this street for about ten minutes, you'll find a bus stop, take No. 21 bus, then it will take you there.

A: By the way, is the ticket expensive?

B: No, the ticket is very cheap.

A: Thank you for telling me.

B: You are welcome.

Dialogue 2

A: Ouch.

B: What happened? Where does it hurt?

A: Your car clashed into my leg.

B: Is it serious?

A: Yes, it's bleeding.

B: Shall I call someone for help?

A: But there is few people here.

B: What should I do?

A: You can call for an ambulance.

B: Yes. I was so nervous and I forgot it.

三、Put the following into English.

1. I have lost my passport. Has anyone turned in one?
2. Have you taken any taxis today?
3. Would you please fill in this lost property report?
4. I suggest you report this to police.
5. Let's look for it carefully. Maybe we can find it.
6. What's your trouble?
7. Has it been treated before?
8. When did the pain start?
9. What diseases have you suffered from before?
10. Do you have any pain in the place where I press?

Unit 7 Room Reservation

一、Complete the following dialogue.

may I help you

May I know how many people will be in the party

What kind of room would you like

How do you plan to arrive at the hotel

Our shuttle bus will be waiting for you at the airport

二、Complete the dialogues with the Chinese prompts.

R: Good morning. Room Reservation. What can I do for you?

G: Good morning. I'd like to book a room.

R: What kind of room would you prefer?

G: I want a room with the lake view.

R: I'm so sorry. We do have free rooms but they are all facing the city, not the lake.

G: Let me think about it. I will call you later.

R: Would you mind giving me your name and telephone number? I will call you back if we have the room facing the lake.

G: That's great. My mane is Zhang Yi and my telephone number is 13640086699.

R: Thank you for calling. Goodbye.

三、Put the following into English.

1. I am afraid, we are fully booked for all kinds of rooms on that night. It is the peak season for traveling now.

2. I am so sorry, we have no vacant room for you. But I can recommend you to Shenyang Hotel where you may get a spare room.

3. Is it possible for you to change your reservation date?

4. A deluxe suite is RMB 1,999 per night, plus 10% service charge.

5. The room with a view of the sea is RMB 2,999.

6. We will send you a fax to confirm the reservation as soon as possible.

7. I'd like to cancel a reservation.

8. We offer free transportation to and from the airport.

9. What kind of room would you like?

10. We look forward to seeing you.

Unit 8   Reception Service

一、Complete the following dialogues.

Dialogue 1

Have you made a reservation, sir

All the rooms are full booked

Would you like me to get in touch with somewhere else for you

Dialogue 2

May I be of assistance

Do you have a reservation

Do you need morning call service

We hope you have enjoyed your stay in the hotel

二、Complete the dialogue with the Chinese prompts.

R: Good evening, sir. May I help you?

G: I want a room in your hotel.

R: Have you made a reservation?

G: No.

R: What kind of room would you like, sir?

G: A standard room.

R: A smoking or non-smoking room?

G: Any extra charge for a smoking room?

R: No, sir.

G: In that case, I want a smoking room. How much do you charge for a standard room per night?

R: RMB 660 per night.

G: Is there any discount if I stay here several days?

R: How long are you going to stay in our hotel?

G: Ten days.

R: Then you will have a 10% discount.

G: Thank you. I will take it.

R: Could you fill in the registration form?

G: OK.

R: Here is your key card. Your room number is 1012. It's on the tenth floor and the bellboy will show you up. Have a nice evening.

三、Put the following into English.

1. If you need anything else, please call room service.

2. Just a moment, please. Let me check the reservation record.

3. Would you mind filling in the registration form and paying RMB 900 in advance, please?

4. How would you like to settle your bill?

5. Here is the receipt. Please keep it.

6. The bellman will show you up with your luggage.

7. In whose name was the reservation made?

8. I'm so sorry, but there is no reservation in your name.

9. May I print your credit card?

10. We hope you have enjoyed your stay in the hotel.

Unit 9　In-house Service

一、**Complete the following dialogue.**

May I help you

To which country

How many pages are they in all

Which one would you prefer

When do you expect to get them, please

二、**Complete the dialogue with the Chinese prompts.**

C: Good morning. How may I help you?

G: I would like to book a one-day city tour.

C: How many is it for?

G: 20.

C: When would you like to go?

G: Tomorrow morning.

C: Do you need a guide to service you all throughout the tour?

G: Yes, please. And the guide must be both capable in English and Germany.

C: No problem. In that case, we charge more.

G: How much does it cost?

C: RMB 200 per person.

G: That's fine. May I see the itinerary?

C: Here is the timetable of our tour. The hotel limousine leaves at 7:00 o'clock tomorrow morning, and returns at around 5:30 tomorrow afternoon.

G: Thank you.

C: Our tour guide will confirm the itinerary with you tonight.

三、**Put the following into English.**

1. Just a moment, please. I will bring a luggage cart.

2. Do you mind if I put your luggage by the wardrobe?

3. That's very kind of you, but I'm afraid we don't accept tips. Thank you all the same.

4. Could you make sure that your bags are packed before you leave?

5. At what time do you want me to call you up?

6. A person-to-person or a station call?

7. Could you put me through to Room 1601, please?

8. For outside calls, please dial 9 first and then dial the number you want.

9. There is no answer. Would you like to leave a message?

10. I am sorry. The guest's extension number is confidential.

Unit 10　Check-out Service

一、**Complete the following dialogues.**

Dialogue 1

Are you a guest of the hotel

What kind of foreign currency have you got, sir

How much would you like to change

How would you like your money

Dialogue 2

May I have your name or room number

Would you like to check and see if the account is correct

How would you like to make payment

May I know the name of your company, please

We look forward to seeing you again

二、**Complete the dialogue with the Chinese prompts.**

C: Good morning, sir. May I help you?

G: I'm Tom Cruise. I've just settled my bill with your colleague. But then I realized that there might be something wrong with the bill.

C: What is it, sir?

G: I didn't make any long calls during my stay but you've charged me three hundred *yuan* for IDD.

C: Just a moment, please. I will check with the department concerned.

G: How long will it take? I am catching a flight.

C: Don't worry, sir. We will check it immediately... I'm sorry, Mr. Cruise. There has been a mistake. Here is the corrected bill and the money that we overcharged you. I'm terribly sorry for the mistake.

G: That's alright as long as I get this straightened out.

C: Thank you very much, Mr. Cruise. We hope you have a good trip.

三、**Put the following into English.**

1. Have you used any hotel services or the mini-bar this morning, sir?

2. Add to my account, please.

3. Five nights at $120 each, and here are the meals that you had at the hotel. That makes a total of $870.

4. Would you like to check and see if the account is correct?

5. That charge is for drinks taken from the mini-bar, sir.

6. The service charge is included in the bill.

7. My company will pay B&B charge, and the other will be paid by myself.

8. Our check-out time is 12:00 at noon, but you used the room until 6:00 pm. We have to charge an extra 50% of the room rate.

9. Would you sign your name here?

10. Here is your change and receipt.

Unit 11　　A La Carte

一、**Complete the following dialogues.**

Dialogue 1

What would you like to drink

With or without ice

How about you

Shall I bring you some snacks

Enjoy your drinks

Dialogue 2

What can I do for you

How many people will there be

How much would you plan to spend for per person

May I know your special requirements

How about table plans

二、**Complete the dialogue with the Chinese prompts.**

W: Good afternoon. Welcome to McDonald's. Do you like any hamburgers?

G: I do not like this one. Do you have any other combo?

W: Yes, we have hamburger combo, chicken combo, Spicy McWings combo. Which do you like?

G: What kind of hamburger do you have?

W: We have chicken hamburgers, beef hamburgers, and fish hamburgers. Which one would you like?

G: Chicken hamburger.

W: Spicy or not Spicy?

G: Not Spicy.

W: Then I suggest you have Grilled Chicken Burger. It is not spicy and only 23 *yuan*.

G: What are in the combo?

W: Hamburger, French fries and coke.

G: OK. This one, please.

W: We have a new kind of McWings with honey sauce. Would you like a pair?

G: No, thank you.

W: It is total 23 *yuan*.

(The customer takes out 30 *yuan* to the guest)

W: Here is your change, seven *yuan*. Please go to the left side to wait. Service will prepare it for you. This is the straw, Please help yourself.

三、Put the following into English.

1. Would you like to order a full meal course or an a la carte?
2. The regular dinners include appetizers, main courses, and desserts.
3. May I serve soup to you now?
4. What would you like with your steak, sir?
5. What kind of salad dressing would you prefer?
6. Do you want your coffee with the meal or with dessert?
7. We serve Carlsberg, Heineken, San Miguel, Kirtin, Foster, Guinness Stout and Budweiser.
8. Would you like to have some snacks with your wine?
9. Brandy on the rocks or straight up?
10. We serve cucumber juice, orange juice, carrot juice and tomato juice. All of them are spot-squashed.

Unit 12   In Chinese Restaurant

一、Complete the following dialogues.

Dialogue 1

Welcome to our restaurant

Do you have a reservation

I'm sorry to say that we haven't got any vacant seat at present

Where would you like to sit

Will this table be all right

Dialogue 2

How would you like to pay

May I print your card, sir

Do you have another card

Could you sign your name here, please

二、Complete the dialogue with the Chinese prompts.

W: Good evening, ladies and gentlemen. A table for six? Would you step this way, please.

G: Thank you.

W: Would you care for a drink first?

G: Yes, please. Two bottles of beer and four cokes.

W: Would you like to order now?

G: What would you recommend?

W: If you like a hot and spicy food, then try Mapo Bean Curd. It is a famous Sichuan dish.

G: Alright. Any other spicy food for us?

W: How about Shredded Beef in Chill Sauce?

G: Great. We take that. Could you give me Beijing Roast Duck, please?

W: Certainly, sir. Would you like some rice or soup?

G: Sweet corn soup and two Yang Zhou Fried Rice, please.

W: The order will be served immediately.

三、Put the following into English.

1. I would like to reserve a table for 8 with a Lazy Susan, please.

2. I'll be back with your order in a little while.

3. Cantonese food is lighter while Sichuan food is spicy and hot.

4. I want Kung Pao Chicken. Will it be served quickly?

5. These are Twice-Cooked Pork Slices, Sweet and Sour Fried Mandarin Fish in Squirrel Shape and Mapo Bean Curd.

6. We have Deep-fried Green Onion Pancakes and Spring Rolls today.

7. This is the complete course. If you would like any additional dishes, please call me.

8. What would you like, Chinese, Western, Japanese or Korean cuisine?

9. How much would you like to spend per head?

10. What about the venue for the function? Indoor or outdoor?

参考文献

1. 陈欣.导游英语情景口语[M].北京:北京大学出版社,2009.
2. 李昕.实用旅游心理学教程[M].北京:中国财政经济出版社,2005.
3. 教育部《旅游英语》编写组.旅游英语[M].北京:高等教育出版社,2002.
4. 南凡.旅游英语[M].北京:高等教育出版社,2005.
5. 杨华.实用旅游英语[M].北京:中国人民大学出版社,2006.
6. 孙小珂.新编饭店英语(修订版)[M].武汉:武汉大学出版社,2007.
7. 谢先泽.中国旅游:英语读本[M].成都:西南财经大学出版社,2006.
8. www.chinapages.com
9. www.ebigear.com